# Mama D's
## Homestyle Italian Cookbook

## Giovanna D'Agostino

Golden Press • New York
Western Publishing Company, Inc.
Racine, Wisconsin

Designed by Remo Cosentino
Photography by Arie deZanger
Illustrated by Frank Bozzo

Special thanks to Hammacher Schlemmer, New York, N.Y., and Plummer McCutcheon, New York, N.Y., for items shown in photographs.

Recipes in this book previously appeared in *Mama D's Italian Cooking...with a Pinch*.
Library of Congress Catalog Card Number: 74-29424
GOLDEN and GOLDEN PRESS® are trademarks of Western Publishing Company, Inc.

# Foreword

This cookbook is my "philosophy" of how to prepare wholesome, homestyle Italian dishes successfully. Fine cooking means simple, tasty food, not necessarily dishes with exotic ingredients or an elaborate cooking process. I have given my recipes to people who had never cooked Italian dishes before. Some of them later told me that they had never realized that cooking could be such fun. In short, cooking need not be a federal case!

I have always made it a point to use ingredients that are easy to get, instead of those found in odd corners of a spice shop or only after much searching around. If a certain herb or spice or ingredient is difficult to find, a new cook can easily lose interest in the recipe. Also, a lot of food normally discarded in cooking, such as celery leaves or the tough parts of the stalks, can be used in good dishes. In other words, "If you waste not, you want not."

I like to use four basic seasonings—salt, pepper, oregano and garlic. (In my cooking classes, I call them SPOGS for short.) Used properly, they will do a very good job. (I should emphasize, though, that oregano, a popular herb, is bitter and should be used very sparingly. Too much oregano can ruin a meal prepared by even the very best cook.)

I want to thank the many dear Italian ladies who taught me how to cook when I was a young married woman. Also, I want to express my thanks to my former landlady, Mrs. Roy Cinquegrani, who taught me how to cook "with a pinch of this and a pinch of that." And I will always be indebted to my sisters-in-law, Rosina and Felicia, who were such excellent cooks and who made me want to stay for supper every time I visited their homes in Chicago. I not only learned their ways of cooking, but also the various Italian dialects. When eventually I visited Italy in the summer of 1970, I found that I had much to be grateful for—from my many friends in both Chicago and Minneapolis.

I hope that this cookbook will enable anyone using it to experience the same joy of cooking that I have had in both my home and my restaurant. It's the willingness to try something new once in a while that can make the simple preparation of a wholesome meal a very rewarding and enriching experience.

Giovanna D'Agostino
(Mama D)

# Contents

# Spicy Braccioli

**BRACCIOLI**

**GREEN BEANS WITH ALMONDS**

**CELERY FRITTERS**

**ORANGE SALAD**

**MAMA D'S HOMEMADE BREAD (PAGE 59)**

**ANISE COOKIES**

*

**SERVES 4 TO 6**

## Braccioli

8 sprigs parsley, chopped
1 clove garlic, minced
½ cup dry bread crumbs
1 tablespoon grated Parmesan cheese
1 small onion, finely chopped
2 hard-cooked eggs, diced
2 strips bacon, diced
1 teaspoon salt
  Pinch of pepper
  Pinch of oregano
1½-pound round steak, pounded on both sides
1 egg, beaten
2 tablespoons flour
¼ cup oil
¾ cup water
  Spaghetti sauce (optional)

Place parsley, garlic, bread crumbs, cheese, onion, hard-cooked eggs, bacon, salt, pepper and oregano in a bowl and mix thoroughly. Lay the steak flat on a table. Spread mixed ingredients on top of steak. Fold edges in and roll. Tie securely with string.

Dip rolled and tied steak in beaten egg, then in flour. Heat oil in a skillet; sauté steak on all sides until golden brown. Place in a roasting pan. Add water and roast in a 350° oven for 45 minutes. Cut into 1½-inch slices and serve as is, or pour spaghetti sauce over the steak, if desired.

## Green Beans with Almonds

2 tablespoons oil
1 onion, finely chopped
1 clove garlic, minced
1 pound fresh green beans, cooked, or 1 (29-ounce) can green beans, drained
  Salt and pepper to taste
2 tablespoons slivered almonds
2 tablespoons grated Parmesan cheese

Heat oil in a skillet; add onion and garlic and sauté until golden brown. Add green beans and cook slowly until hot. Season with salt and pepper. Stir in almonds and sprinkle with cheese just before serving.

Note: For variety, mushrooms may be included; add to pan along with the beans.

6

## Celery Fritters

5 celery stalks (with leaves)
1 cup flour
2 eggs, beaten
   Salt, pepper and oregano
   to taste
1 clove garlic, minced
¼ cup water
¼ cup grated Parmesan cheese
1 cup oil

Wash and chop celery into ½-inch pieces. Add flour, eggs, salt, pepper, oregano, garlic, water and cheese and mix well. It will have the consistency of pancake batter.

Heat oil in a skillet. When hot, drop batter by tablespoonfuls into the oil and fry until golden brown. Drain on paper towels.

## Orange Salad

1 head lettuce
   Salt and pepper to taste
1 tablespoon oil
   Juice of 2 oranges

Break lettuce into pieces. Season to taste with salt and pepper. Mix oil with orange juice. Drizzle over lettuce. Toss gently and serve.

## Anise Cookies

4 eggs
1 cup sugar
1 teaspoon vanilla
⅓ cup milk
2 tablespoons anise seed
3 to 4 cups flour
4 teaspoons baking powder
1 cup shortening

Preheat oven to 375°. Beat eggs well. Add sugar, vanilla, milk and anise seed. Mix well again. In another bowl, mix 3 cups flour, the baking powder and shortening; add liquid mixture. You may have to add more flour or milk to make a cookie-dough consistency. Roll out and cut into desired shapes on a lightly floured board.

Bake on greased cookie sheets for about 12 minutes. Makes 6 to 8 dozen cookies.

❝Be sure you *taste* when you're cooking. If you don't taste, how will you know? If it doesn't taste good to you, don't serve it to anyone else! We all have different taste buds—you can't please everyone. Generally, though, if it tastes good to you and if you are a judge of good food and if you like to eat, you'll know when it's good or bad.❞

# Fried Chicken Italian Style

**FRIED CHICKEN**

**ITALIAN-STYLE NEW POTATOES**

**ZUCCHINI FRITTERS**

**ARTICHOKE-OLIVE SALAD**

**RICOTTA PUDDING**

\*

**SERVES 4**

## Fried Chicken

- 1 teaspoon salt
- ½ teaspoon pepper
- ⅛ teaspoon oregano
- 2 cloves garlic, minced
- 2 cups dry bread crumbs
- ¼ cup grated Parmesan cheese
- 2 eggs
- ¼ cup milk
- 1 frying chicken, cut into serving pieces
- ¼ cup oil

Mix salt, pepper, oregano, garlic, bread crumbs and cheese. Beat eggs and milk. Dip the chicken pieces in the egg-milk mixture, then roll in seasoned bread crumbs. Heat oil in a skillet and fry the chicken pieces over medium heat until golden brown. Place in a roasting pan and bake, uncovered, at 375° for 45 minutes.

## Italian-Style New Potatoes

- 8 new potatoes, cooked
- ¼ cup oil
- 1 teaspoon salt
- ½ teaspoon pepper
- ¼ teaspoon oregano
- 1 clove garlic, minced
- ¼ cup grated Parmesan cheese
- 1 tablespoon chopped parsley

Peel potatoes and leave whole. Put potatoes in a bowl; add oil, salt, pepper, oregano and garlic. Toss together gently. Sprinkle with cheese and parsley.

## Zucchini Fritters

- 2 medium zucchini (unpeeled), sliced paper thin
- 1 cup flour
- 2 eggs, beaten
  Salt, pepper and oregano to taste
- 1 clove garlic, minced
- ¼ cup water
- ¼ cup grated Parmesan cheese
- 1 cup oil

Combine zucchini, flour, eggs, salt, pepper, oregano, garlic, water and cheese; mix thoroughly. Mixture will be the consistency of pancake batter. Heat oil in a skillet. When hot, drop batter by tablespoonfuls into the oil and fry until golden brown. Drain on paper towels.

## Artichoke-Olive Salad

1 (14-ounce) can artichoke hearts, drained
12 pitted black olives
2 teaspoons capers
1 (2-ounce) can anchovies, drained and chopped
2 stalks celery, cut into pieces
1 (4-ounce) jar pimientos, drained and chopped
2 hard-cooked eggs, sliced
1 small onion, minced
1 clove garlic, minced
¼ teaspoon pepper
⅛ teaspoon oregano
1 teaspoon lemon juice
1 tablespoon wine vinegar
¼ cup oil

Put all ingredients in a bowl and toss. Taste for seasoning. Can be chilled.

## Ricotta Pudding

¾ pound ricotta cheese
¼ cup semisweet chocolate chips
¼ cup chopped pecans
3 tablespoons whipping cream
¼ cup chopped maraschino cherries
¼ teaspoon cinnamon
2 tablespoons sugar
4 maraschino cherries

Cream the ricotta and add all other ingredients except whole cherries. Mix thoroughly. Spoon into sherbet glasses. Garnish each serving with a whole maraschino cherry.

66 A gourmet cook is someone who cooks a potato and makes it taste good. Adding fancy wines you never heard of to a dish won't make you a gourmet cook. 99

# Feast From the Sea

BAKED POMPANO
PIEDMONT-STYLE RICE
BEET AND ONION SALAD
PEARS WITH RED WINE
RUM BALLS

*

SERVES 4

## Baked Pompano

3 to 3½ pounds pompano
2 eggs
1 teaspoon salt
½ teaspoon pepper
⅛ teaspoon oregano
1 clove garlic, minced
1 cup dry bread crumbs
½ cup grated Parmesan cheese
4 sprigs parsley, chopped
4 tablespoons butter
½ cup dry white wine
Lemon wedges

Have pompano cut into 8 fillets. Rinse and pat dry with paper towels. Beat eggs in a shallow dish. Mix salt, pepper, oregano, garlic, bread crumbs, cheese and parsley together. Dip fillets in eggs, then in bread crumb mixture. Lay fillets in greased baking dish and dot with butter. Pour on wine and bake in a 375° oven for 15 to 20 minutes. Serve with lemon wedges.

## Piedmont-Style Rice

2 small onions, minced
4 tablespoons butter
¼ pound prosciutto ham or chicken giblets, finely chopped
½ cup sliced mushrooms
2 cups uncooked rice
2 quarts hot beef or chicken stock
Pinch of salt
½ teaspoon pepper
½ teaspoon nutmeg
½ cup grated Parmesan cheese

Sauté onions in butter over medium heat until lightly browned. Add prosciutto or giblets, mushrooms, half the rice and about half the stock. Continue stirring while adding remaining rice and stock. Cook until rice is tender. Rice should be moist but not too wet. Season with salt, pepper and nutmeg. Sprinkle with cheese.

## Beet and Onion Salad

1 (29-ounce) can sliced beets, drained
1 large onion, sliced and separated into rings
Salt and pepper to taste
⅛ teaspoon garlic salt
Pinch of oregano
2 tablespoons oil
1 tablespoon wine vinegar
½ teaspoon sugar

Put beets in a bowl. Add onion rings, salt, pepper, garlic salt and oregano. Mix oil, vinegar and sugar in a bottle. Shake well and drizzle over the salad. Chill in refrigerator at least 1 hour before serving.

## Pears with Red Wine

½ cup sugar
½ cup water
1 stick cinnamon
½ cup Italian red wine
2 fresh pears, pared

Heat sugar, water, cinnamon stick and wine to boiling. Lower heat; boil for 10 to 12 minutes, stirring occasionally. Cut the pears in half, add to the syrup and simmer 15 minutes. Place pears in sherbet glasses and pour a little wine syrup over each. You may top with whipped cream and garnish each with a maraschino cherry.

## Rum Balls

2 cups chocolate cookie crumbs (e.g., chocolate wafers)
2 cups confectioners' sugar
1 cup ground almonds or pecans
1 cup chopped almonds or pecans
¼ cup cocoa
¼ cup rum (light or dark)
3 tablespoons corn syrup
¼ cup granulated sugar

Combine cookie crumbs, confectioners' sugar, ground nuts, chopped nuts and cocoa. Mix thoroughly with hands. Mix rum and corn syrup; pour into dry ingredients. Mix thoroughly. Pinch off pieces and roll into balls the size of a walnut. Then roll in granulated sugar. Put into tightly covered container and refrigerate for 2 days before serving. Makes 4 dozen balls.

66 Some domestic American cheeses are better than the imports. Whenever you can, taste the cheese before you buy. Sometimes I've tasted both domestic and imported Provolone—and ended up buying the domestic, which costs quite a bit less. If the cheese is prepackaged, you'll have to take a chance on it. 99

# A Roman Dinner

**VEAL SCALOPPINE**
**FINGER CROQUETTES**
**SAUTEED ASPARAGUS**
**LETTUCE, PEAR
AND NUT SALAD**
**CENCI COOKIES**

*

**SERVES 6**

## Veal Scaloppine

1½  pounds veal (cut from the
    leg or shoulder), thinly
    sliced and cut into 6 serving
    pieces
 ¼  teaspoon oregano
 1  clove garlic, minced
    Salt and pepper to taste
    Flour for dredging
 ¼  cup oil
 2  tablespoons butter
 1  cup white wine
 6  slices prosciutto ham
 6  slices mozzarella cheese
 ½  cup grated Parmesan cheese

Season veal with oregano, garlic,
salt and pepper; roll in flour. Heat
oil and butter in a skillet and sauté
veal quickly on both sides until
light golden brown. Transfer to a
baking dish. Add wine to fat remaining in the pan and simmer for
a few minutes. Pour over veal in
baking dish. Place 1 slice of ham
and 1 slice of mozzarella cheese
on each slice of veal. Sprinkle with
Parmesan cheese. Bake in a
400° oven until cheese is melted.
Serve hot.

## Finger Croquettes

 3  cups mashed potatoes
 ¼  cup grated Parmesan cheese
 ½  cup flour
 ½  cup bread crumbs
 3  eggs, beaten
    Pinch of oregano
 2  cloves garlic, minced
    Salt and pepper to taste
    Oil for frying

Mix all ingredients except oil.
Shape into fingers (croquettes).
Heat 1 inch of oil in a 6- to 8-inch
skillet. Test heat of oil by dropping
a bread cube into it. Oil is hot
enough when cube browns
quickly. Fry croquettes until gold-
en brown on all sides. Serve hot.

## Sautéed Asparagus

 ¼  cup butter
 ½  cup bread crumbs
 2  pounds fresh asparagus,
    cooked, or 2 (16-ounce) cans
    asparagus spears, heated and
    drained
    Pinch of salt
 ¼  teaspoon pepper
 ¼  teaspoon garlic powder
 1  hard-cooked egg, sieved
 ¼  cup grated Romano cheese

Melt butter in saucepan. Add
bread crumbs and sauté until gold-
en brown. Sprinkle over hot
cooked asparagus. Sprinkle with
salt, pepper and garlic powder;
toss gently. Sprinkle with egg and
cheese.

## Lettuce, Pear and Nut Salad

3 tablespoons oil
Juice of 1 large lemon
3 fresh pears, peeled and quartered
1 large head lettuce, broken into pieces
¾ cup chopped walnuts

Heat oil and lemon juice together, but do not bring to a boil. Mix pears, lettuce and nuts together; gently toss. Pour oil and lemon mixture over all. Chill and serve.

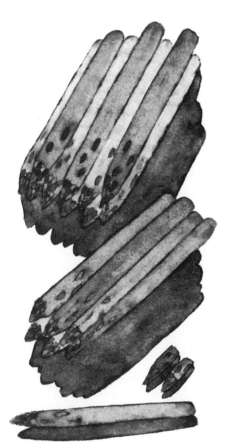

## Cenci Cookies

2 cups flour
2 tablespoons butter
5 teaspoons sugar
3 eggs, beaten
1 teaspoon salt
Grated rind of 1 lemon
3 tablespoons wine (red or white)
Oil for deep frying
Confectioners' sugar

Put flour in a bowl and cut in butter. Add sugar, eggs, salt, lemon rind and wine. Work everything together and knead well. Cover bowl with a damp cloth. Roll out about ¼ of the dough at a time into a rectangle shape and cut into strips with a ravioli cutter or knife. Shape by tying into loose knots. Fry in deep fat; drain well on paper towels. Cool and sprinkle with confectioners' sugar. Makes about 4 dozen cookies.

66 You don't need a fancy electric deep fryer. Pour oil into a heavy skillet to a 1-inch depth and heat it. Test the temperature of the oil by throwing a bread cube into the pan. When the cube browns rapidly to a golden brown, the oil is hot enough for frying your food. 99

# Good—
# and Good
# for You!

ITALIAN-STYLE LIVER

PASTA SHELLS WITH
PEAS AND TOMATOES

ONION AND TOMATO SALAD
WITH ROQUEFORT CHEESE

BREAD AND BUTTER

CHERRIES IN WINE

*

SERVES 4 TO 6

## Italian-Style Liver

4 to 6 slices beef liver
  Salt to taste
⅛ teaspoon pepper
½ cup flour
2 tablespoons oil
4 to 6 strips bacon
2 or 3 small onions, sliced and
  separated into rings
1 clove garlic, minced
1 (4-ounce) can mushrooms
  (undrained)
¼ cup water

Season liver slices with salt and pepper. Dredge in flour on both sides and set aside. Heat oil in a skillet and fry the bacon until crisp, then drain on paper towels. Add onions and garlic to oil and bacon fat in skillet; sauté until golden brown. Remove from skillet. Sauté liver on both sides, turning only once. Add bacon strips, onions, garlic, mushrooms and water. Cover and simmer over low heat for 30 minutes.

## Pasta Shells with Peas and Tomatoes

¼ cup oil
2 small onions, chopped
2 cloves garlic, minced
1 teaspoon salt
½ teaspoon pepper
⅛ teaspoon oregano
2 small raw potatoes, peeled
  and cubed
1 (29-ounce) can peas
  (undrained)
½ cup canned tomatoes,
  crushed, or 2 fresh tomatoes,
  crushed
½ cup grated Parmesan cheese
6 quarts water
1 tablespoon salt
1 pound pasta shells (smallest
  size available)

Heat oil in a large saucepan. Add onions, garlic, 1 teaspoon salt, the pepper and oregano and sauté until garlic is light golden brown. Add cubed potatoes and stir gently for 10 minutes; then add peas, tomatoes and cheese. Simmer for 1 hour over medium heat.

Bring water and 1 tablespoon salt to rolling boil; add pasta shells and cook until *just* tender (don't overcook). Drain in a colander and set aside until sauce is done. Add shells to sauce and simmer for 10 minutes. More Parmesan cheese may be used to top each serving.

14

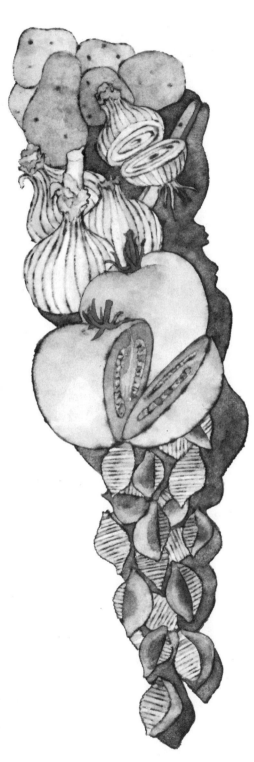

## Onion and Tomato Salad with Roquefort Cheese

1 onion, finely chopped
4 tomatoes, quartered
1 (2-ounce) package Roquefort
  cheese, crumbled
  Salt to taste
¼ teaspoon pepper
⅛ teaspoon oregano
¼ cup oil
1 tablespoon vinegar

Combine onion, tomatoes, cheese, salt, pepper and oregano in a salad bowl. Sprinkle with oil and vinegar. Toss lightly.

## Cherries in Wine

1 (29-ounce) can pitted tart
  red cherries (undrained)
1¼ cups sugar
2 or 3 cups red wine
  (dry or sweet)
1 cup whipping cream,
  whipped stiff
  Maraschino cherries

Put tart cherries in a saucepan; mix in sugar and wine. Bring to a boil over low heat. Lower heat and simmer for 30 minutes. Pour into parfait glasses; top with whipped cream and garnish each with a maraschino cherry.

66 I cook like your grandmothers did when they came to this country. No fancy utensils. And this is the way I teach my cooking classes. I've heard so many comments from young girls saying, "Oh gosh, my grandmother makes this or that and it's so good, but she can't tell me how to make it. What is a pinch?" And I tell them there are two kinds of pinches—one you see and one you feel. I love to season everything. Proper seasoning makes all the difference between good food and bad food. 99

# Dinner From Your Garden

**STUFFED PEPPERS**

**BAKED POTATOES WITH MOZZARELLA CHEESE**

**ZUCCHINI WITH ONIONS**

**FRESH MUSHROOM SALAD**

**PARMESAN GARLIC BREAD (PAGE 23)**

**STRAWBERRY ICE**

*

**SERVES 4**

## Stuffed Peppers

8 medium green peppers
1 pound ground beef
2 cloves garlic, minced
3 or 4 sprigs parsley, chopped
4 slices dried bread, moistened in water and squeezed
2 eggs
  Salt, pepper and oregano to taste
  Tomato sauce (optional)

Clean peppers for stuffing by cutting off tops and removing seeds. Place ground beef, garlic, parsley, bread, eggs, salt, pepper and oregano in a bowl and mix well. Stuff peppers with meat mixture. Place peppers in a greased roasting pan and bake for 30 to 40 minutes in a 300° oven. Tomato sauce may be spooned over peppers if desired.

## Baked Potatoes with Mozzarella Cheese

4 baking potatoes
  Oil
  Salt, pepper, oregano and garlic salt to taste
  Milk
  Butter
¼ cup grated Parmesan cheese
4 slices mozzarella cheese

Wash, scrub and oil each potato well. Bake in a 375° oven for 1 hour. Test with a fork to see if potatoes are soft. Remove from oven and cut a slice off each potato. Scoop potatoes into a mixing bowl, reserving skins. Mash well, adding salt, pepper, oregano and garlic salt. Add a little milk and butter and 2 tablespoons of the Parmesan cheese; beat until fluffy. Refill potato shells and sprinkle with remaining Parmesan cheese. Put a thin slice of mozzarella cheese on each potato. Place potatoes on a baking sheet and return to oven until cheese melts, about 15 minutes.

16

## Zucchini with Onions

¼ cup oil
3 medium zucchini, thinly sliced
2 small onions, thinly sliced
Salt, pepper and oregano to taste
1 clove garlic, minced
2 tablespoons wine vinegar (optional)
2 tablespoons grated Parmesan cheese

Heat oil in a skillet. Add zucchini and onions and sauté slowly. Add salt, pepper, oregano and garlic and cook until zucchini is tender. Stir in wine vinegar if you like (it adds a little more flavor). Before serving, sprinkle with cheese.

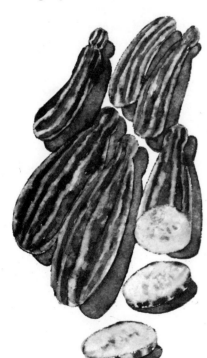

## Fresh Mushroom Salad

1 pound fresh mushrooms, thinly sliced
2 small onions or scallions, minced
Salt to taste
¼ teaspoon pepper
⅛ teaspoon oregano
1 clove garlic, minced
1 teaspoon lemon juice

Put all the ingredients into a serving bowl and toss. Taste for seasoning. Chill before serving.

## Strawberry Ice

1 pint fresh strawberries
¾ cup sugar
1 cup boiling water
2 tablespoons lemon juice
Whipped cream (optional)
Maraschino cherries (optional)

Wash and hull strawberries and put through a food mill. Add sugar to boiling water, stir to dissolve and cool. Combine strawberry puree, sugar-water syrup and lemon juice. Pour into refrigerator tray and put in freezer until firm. Serve in sherbet glasses and top each with a bit of whipped cream and a cherry.

66 Can you run a car on water instead of gasoline? The body is the same way. You have to have the essential foods God put on earth—and the potato is one of them. So if you're on a diet, instead of eating a whole potato, eat half or a quarter. But have it, and serve it to your family once in a while. It's really sad. You go to somebody's home and they don't have any potatoes. But they do have that packaged stuff you add water to and stir. 99

# Luncheon in Venice

**VENETIAN RISOTTO**

**TOMATOES STUFFED WITH CHICKEN SALAD**

**SAUTEED GARLIC BREAD**

**COFFEE ICE CREAM (PAGE 91)**

\*

**SERVES 4**

## Venetian Risotto

¼ cup butter
2 chicken gizzards, cut up
2 chicken livers, cut up
2 cloves garlic, minced
1 small onion, chopped
1 (6-ounce) can tomato paste
2 (6-ounce) cans water
  Pinch of salt
¼ teaspoon pepper
⅛ teaspoon oregano
½ teaspoon cinnamon
6 cups chicken broth
2 cups uncooked rice
½ cup grated Parmesan cheese

Heat butter in a saucepan. Add all ingredients except broth, rice and cheese. Simmer slowly for 45 minutes. Heat broth to boiling point in a large pot. Add simmered mixture and rice, a little at a time, until all ingredients are combined. Cook until rice is tender. Stir in cheese. Serve immediately.

## Tomatoes Stuffed with Chicken Salad

4 large tomatoes
⅔ cup mayonnaise
1 cup diced cooked chicken
3 sprigs parsley, chopped
1 cup diced celery
1 small onion, finely chopped
1 clove garlic, minced
  Pinch of salt
¼ teaspoon pepper
  Paprika
  Lettuce leaves

Cut tops from tomatoes and scoop out pulp. Combine all remaining ingredients (include tomato pulp, if you wish) except paprika and lettuce. Toss together gently. Fill tomatoes with mixture and garnish each with a sprinkle of paprika. Serve on lettuce leaves.

## Sautéed Garlic Bread

8 slices day-old bread
  Butter
½ teaspoon garlic powder
¼ cup grated Parmesan cheese

Butter bread on both sides. Brown in heavy skillet on both sides until golden brown. Sprinkle with garlic powder and cheese. Serve hot.

## Clam Soup

2 tablespoons oil
1 clove garlic, minced
1 onion, chopped
½ cup dry wine (red or white)
4 cups tomatoes (fresh or canned), coarsely chopped
8 to 10 sprigs parsley, chopped
2 (7-ounce) cans minced clams (undrained)
1 teaspoon salt
¼ teaspoon pepper
⅛ teaspoon oregano
¼ cup grated Parmesan cheese
2 quarts boiling water

Heat oil in a 4- to 6-quart pot. Add garlic and onion and sauté. Add wine, tomatoes, parsley, clams, salt, pepper and oregano. Simmer, covered, for 20 minutes. Add cheese and boiling water. Simmer, uncovered, for 45 minutes. Serve immediately. (Refrigerate remaining soup.)

## Tuna Fish and White Bean Salad

2 cups canned white beans
¼ cup oil
1 tablespoon lemon juice
¼ teaspoon pepper
2 small onions, chopped
2 sprigs parsley, chopped
1 (6-ounce) can tuna fish (undrained)
1 clove garlic, minced
Pinch of salt

Drain beans well; place in a serving bowl. Add oil, lemon juice, pepper, onions, parsley, tuna fish, garlic and salt. Toss gently.

## Almond Ricotta Cheese Fritters

½ pound almond macaroons, finely crushed in blender
1 pound ricotta cheese
2 tablespoons granulated sugar
½ teaspoon cinnamon
3 eggs, beaten
1 cup flour
1 egg, beaten
2 cups dry bread crumbs
1½ cups oil
Confectioners' sugar

Place the macaroons, ricotta, granulated sugar, cinnamon, 3 beaten eggs and flour in a bowl; mix well. Then flour your hands and roll the mixture into balls. Dip in 1 beaten egg and coat with bread crumbs. Heat oil in a skillet and fry a few fritters at a time. Remove with a slotted spoon and sprinkle with confectioners' sugar. Serve hot or cold. Makes 3 to 4 dozen fritters.

# A Seafood Supper

**CLAM SOUP**

**TUNA FISH AND WHITE BEAN SALAD**

**BREAD AND BUTTER**

**ALMOND RICOTTA CHEESE FRITTERS**

\*

**SERVES 4**

# An Easy Oven Barbecue

**BARBECUED SPARERIBS WITH DRESSING**

**ROMANO FRIED POTATOES**

**ASPARAGUS MILAN STYLE**

**BREAD AND BUTTER**

**FROSTED GRAPES**

*

**SERVES 6**

## Barbecued Spareribs with Dressing

3  cups bread crumbs
2  small onions, chopped
2  cloves garlic, minced
2  eggs, beaten
1  stalk celery, chopped
6  sprigs parsley, chopped
½  cup grated Romano cheese
   Salt to taste
½  teaspoon pepper
¼  teaspoon oregano
3  to 4 pounds spareribs (2 sides of ribs)
   Barbecue Sauce (right)

Mix together all ingredients except spareribs and Barbecue Sauce. Spread on one side of ribs. Place other side of ribs on top and tie securely with string. Place in a baking dish and brown in a 375° oven for 20 minutes on each side.

When golden brown, pour Barbecue Sauce over the ribs. Lower heat to 350°, cover baking dish with aluminum foil and bake for 1½ to 2 hours, or until ribs are tender.

## Barbecue Sauce

2  tablespoons oil
2  onions, diced
2  cloves garlic, minced
   Salt to taste
½  teaspoon pepper
   Juice of 1 lemon
1  cup water
3  tablespoons brown sugar
1  (29-ounce) can tomatoes, crushed

Heat oil and sauté onions and garlic for a few minutes. Add salt, pepper, lemon juice, water and brown sugar. Add tomatoes and simmer together for 30 minutes.

## Romano Fried Potatoes

¼  cup bread crumbs
¼  cup grated Romano cheese
    Pinch of salt
¼  teaspoon pepper
⅛  teaspoon oregano
1  clove garlic, minced
    Oil for deep frying
4  large Idaho potatoes, peeled
    and cut into lengthwise strips
2  eggs, beaten

Mix bread crumbs, cheese, salt, pepper, oregano and garlic. Heat oil to 375°. Dip potato strips into beaten eggs, then into bread crumb mixture. Fry until golden brown on all sides. Put in a baking dish and bake in a 350° oven for at least 30 minutes or until tender. Serve hot.

## Asparagus Milan Style

1  bunch (about 1 pound) fresh
    asparagus, trimmed
    Butter
3  eggs
    Pinch of salt
¼  teaspoon pepper
1  clove garlic, minced
½  cup grated Romano cheese

Cook asparagus in boiling salted water for about 10 minutes, or until barely tender. Drain and put in a buttered baking dish. Beat eggs with salt, pepper and garlic. Pour over asparagus. Sprinkle with cheese. Bake, uncovered, in a 350° oven for about 20 minutes or until eggs are set.

## Frosted Grapes

½  cup water
½  cup sugar
1½  pounds grapes (any kind)
    Sugar

Mix water and ½ cup sugar together in saucepan; boil for 6 to 7 minutes. Dip clusters of grapes in syrup; sprinkle with additional sugar. Put on rack until sugar hardens. Cool and serve.

**66** Personally, I like Romano better than Parmesan cheese. It has a little more taste and body to it. When you add Romano cheese to something, you know it's *there*. It's a little sharper. I always buy my cheese in chunks and wrap each chunk in a damp cloth before storing it in the refrigerator. If the cloth is kept moist, the cheese won't dry out. **99**

# Everybody Loves Lasagne

**BAKED LASAGNE**
**ROMAINE SALAD**
**PARMESAN GARLIC BREAD**
**SICILIAN FRUIT PLATE**
*
**SERVES 4 TO 6**

## Baked Lasagne

6 quarts water
1 tablespoon salt
1 pound lasagne noodles
  Lasagne Sauce (right)
  Lasagne Filling (right)
¾ cup coarsely grated Romano cheese
½ pound mozzarella cheese, coarsely grated

Bring water and salt to rolling boil in large pot. Add lasagne noodles and cook until just tender—do not overcook. Remove from heat and run cold water into pot until noodles are cold, then drain.

Use an oblong baking dish at least 2½ to 3 inches deep (a cake pan will do). Grease baking dish; cover the bottom with some of the Lasagne Sauce and 2 tablespoons water. Add a layer of drained noodles, a layer of Lasagne Filling and then a thin layer of sauce. Sprinkle with part of the grated Romano and mozzarella cheeses. Repeat layers, finishing off with noodles on the top. Pour more sauce over the top and sprinkle with remaining grated Romano and mozzarella cheeses. Cover with aluminum foil and bake in a 375° oven for 60 to 70 minutes.

## Lasagne Sauce

½ cup oil
2 medium onions, finely chopped
2 cloves garlic, minced
  Salt to taste
½ teaspoon pepper
¼ teaspoon oregano
1 (6-ounce) can tomato paste
1 (6-ounce) can water
2 (29-ounce) cans Italian tomatoes, crushed

Heat oil. Add onions and garlic; cook until brown. Add salt, pepper, oregano, tomato paste, water and tomatoes. Simmer, uncovered, for 1½ hours, stirring occasionally.

Note: Any sauce left over may be served on spaghetti.

## Lasagne Filling

1 pound lean ground beef
1 pound ricotta cheese
¾ cup grated Romano cheese
3 eggs
  Pinch of salt
½ teaspoon pepper
2 cloves garlic, minced
¼ teaspoon oregano

Put all ingredients in a mixing bowl and mix well.

## Romaine Salad

1 head romaine lettuce
   Salt and pepper to taste
1 clove garlic, minced
¼ cup oil
1½ tablespoons wine vinegar

Wash romaine leaves and pat dry with paper towels. Tear leaves into bite-size pieces. Place in salad bowl. Add all other ingredients and toss gently.

## Parmesan Garlic Bread

1 loaf French bread
   Butter
   Garlic powder
   Grated Parmesan cheese

Cut the bread into 1½-inch-thick slices, but do not cut all the way through. Butter each slice on both sides. Sprinkle lightly with garlic powder and cheese. Wrap in aluminum foil and bake in a 375° oven for 25 minutes.

## Sicilian Fruit Plate

Arrange a selection of sliced fresh fruit (your choice) on a platter. Drizzle kirsch over the fruit and chill for at least 1 hour before serving.

66 Of course you should arrange your menus and your food with eye appeal in mind. But don't get carried away—some people in my cooking classes are overly concerned with how food *looks*. Be sure your food tastes good. In this respect, food is like a person—inner beauty is much more important. 99

# To Welcome Spring

ROAST LAMB SICILIAN STYLE

BOILED POTATOES WITH
PARSLEY

GREEN BEANS WITH
TOMATOES (PAGE 41)

LENTIL SALAD

STRAWBERRIES IN WINE

*

SERVES 6

## Roast Lamb Sicilian Style

2  slices prosciutto ham, diced
1  teaspoon rosemary
   Salt and pepper to taste
2  or 3 sprigs parsley,
   chopped
2  cloves garlic, minced
3- to 3½-pound leg of lamb
   Enough Romano cheese slices
   (½x½ inch) to fill slits
   Oil
   Oregano to taste
   Garlic powder
1  cup water

Mix together ham, rosemary, salt, pepper, parsley and garlic. Wipe leg of lamb. Cut slits all over with sharp knife. Stuff each slit with ham mixture. Push a cheese slice into each slit. Rub lamb with oil. Rub salt, pepper, oregano and garlic powder over both sides. Place in greased baking pan and add the water. Roast in a 375° oven for approximately 30 minutes per pound (until tender), basting occasionally.

## Boiled Potatoes with Parsley

12  small new potatoes
    Salt, pepper and oregano
 1  clove garlic, minced
 ¼  cup grated Romano cheese
 ¼  cup oil
 2  sprigs parsley, finely chopped

Boil and peel potatoes. Put in a bowl and season with salt, pepper, oregano, garlic and cheese. Add oil and parsley. Toss gently. Serve hot or cold.

## Lentil Salad

1  cup dried lentils
1  small onion, finely chopped
1  small bay leaf
2  stalks celery, diced
2  small onions, finely chopped
2  sprigs parsley, chopped
3  small tomatoes, quartered
1  tablespoon wine vinegar
5  tablespoons oil
¼  teaspoon pepper
1  clove garlic, minced
⅛  teaspoon oregano
   Salt to taste
   Grated Romano or Parmesan cheese

Put lentils, 1 onion and the bay leaf in a saucepan. Add water and simmer until lentils are tender. Drain; discard bay leaf. Put lentils in salad bowl. Add all other ingredients except cheese and toss gently. Sprinkle with cheese.

## Strawberries in Wine

1  quart fresh strawberries,
   hulled and washed
3  tablespoons sugar
⅔  cup Marsala wine or sauterne

Gently toss strawberries and sugar in a bowl. Pour wine over berries. Chill; serve in sherbet glasses.

## Spaghetti with Garlic and Oil

6 quarts water
  Salt
1 pound spaghetti
5 cloves garlic, minced
¼ cup oil
6 or 7 sprigs parsley, finely chopped
¼ teaspoon pepper
¼ cup grated Romano cheese

Bring water and 1 tablespoon salt to rolling boil in large pot. Add spaghetti and cook until *al dente*. While spaghetti is cooking, sauté garlic in oil in a saucepan. Add parsley, salt to taste and the pepper. Drain spaghetti and place on a platter. Pour hot sauce over spaghetti and mix well. Sprinkle cheese over all. Serve hot.

## Mama D's Homemade Sausage

1½ pounds fresh pork butt, coarsely ground
  Pinch of crushed red pepper
  Fennel seed to taste
  Salt to taste
  Sausage casing, one inch in diameter*

Mix ground pork, red pepper, fennel and salt together and let stand for 20 minutes. Soak casing in lukewarm water and wash well. Using a funnel with a long neck, slip casing over the end and tie firmly with string. Tie end of casing. Then, holding the casing firmly, spoon meat into the funnel, pushing it into the casing a little at a time. Fill casing firmly. Make sausage lengths as long as you like and tie together. Prick the sausages with a needle. Fry or broil until thoroughly cooked. If you prefer, you can bake the sausages in a 375° oven for at least 45 minutes. Be sure pork is thoroughly cooked.

*Pork casings are the best—but ask your butcher for suggestions.

Note: Uncooked sausages can be made ahead and refrigerated for later use. You can use this recipe to make sausage patties, also (omit casing).

# Lots of Garlic!

**SPAGHETTI WITH GARLIC AND OIL**

**MAMA D'S HOMEMADE SAUSAGE**

**ARTICHOKE-OLIVE SALAD (PAGE 9)**

**LEMON ICE (PAGE 53)**

*

**SERVES 4 TO 6**

# Chop Suey Italian Style

**MAMA D'S CHOP SUEY**

**RICE**

**ITALIAN COLESLAW**

**BREAD AND BUTTER**

**CARAMEL PUDDING**

\*

**SERVES 6**

### Mama D's Chop Suey

1 bunch celery, with leaves
¼ cup oil
½ pound pork, cut into small cubes
½ pound veal, cut into small cubes
½ pound beef, cut into small cubes
4 large onions, sliced and separated into rings
Salt to taste
½ teaspoon pepper
¼ teaspoon oregano
2 cloves garlic, minced
1 (16-ounce) can bean sprouts (undrained)
1 (4-ounce) can mushrooms (undrained)
1 (4-ounce) can water chestnuts, sliced
1 tablespoon soy sauce

Cut celery into ¼-inch pieces. Heat oil in a large saucepan. Add pork, veal and beef. Sauté for 5 minutes. Add onions, celery, salt, pepper, oregano and garlic. Stir and cook for 10 minutes. Add bean sprouts, mushrooms, water chestnuts and soy sauce. Cook over low heat for about 1 hour and 15 minutes, until meat is done. Serve over rice.

### Rice

1 cup uncooked rice
2 cups cold water
1 tablespoon butter

Wash rice in cold water. Pour rice into saucepan. Add 2 cups cold water. Bring to a boil. Add butter. Lower heat to simmer, cover and cook until all water is absorbed. Fluff rice with fork and keep warm over warm water, covered, until ready to serve.

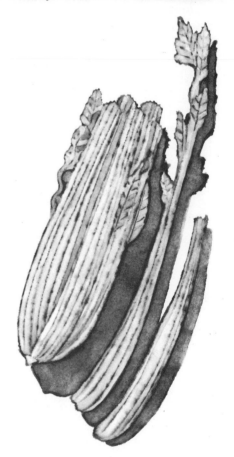

26

## Italian Coleslaw

¼ cup vegetable oil
¼ cup red wine vinegar
1 clove garlic, minced
1 small onion, finely chopped
1 teaspoon sugar
1 (2-ounce) can anchovies
1 small head cabbage, shredded
1 small carrot, grated

Put oil, vinegar, garlic, onion and sugar into a saucepan and bring to a boil. Simmer for 1 minute. Remove from heat and add anchovies. Place cabbage and carrot in a bowl. Pour the liquid mixture over the vegetables and toss lightly; refrigerate.

## Caramel Pudding

1¾ cups sugar
4 cups milk
7 eggs
1 teaspoon salt
2 teaspoons vanilla

Caramelize 1 cup sugar in a heavy skillet over low heat. Pour into a warm 1½-quart mold, coating all sides. Scald milk and cool slightly. Beat eggs. Blend in ¾ cup sugar, salt and vanilla. Mix in milk, a little at a time. Strain mixture into the coated mold. Place in pan of cold water and bake in a preheated 325° oven for 1 to 1½ hours. Insert a knife in the center. If it comes out clean, pudding is done. Refrigerate for at least 1 hour before serving. Invert on serving plate to unmold.

66 All women are good cooks, but they're afraid. The worst thing that ever happened to American women was when they invented the measuring cup. You become so conscious of a fourth of this and an eighth of that. Just learn to know what goes well together and if you like something, don't be afraid to put it in. 99

# For Gourmet Friends

**FETTUCCINE WITH
BUTTER SAUCE**

**BAKED FILLET OF FLOUNDER**

**SAUTEED ASPARAGUS
(PAGE 12)**

**BIBB LETTUCE SALAD
WITH GRAPES**

**RICOTTA PIE**

*

**SERVES 4**

## Fettuccine with Butter Sauce

6 quarts water
1 tablespoon salt
1 pound fettuccine
½ cup (¼ pound) butter
  Salt to taste
¼ teaspoon pepper
⅛ teaspoon oregano
2 cloves garlic, minced
½ cup grated Parmesan cheese

Bring water and 1 tablespoon salt to a rolling boil in a large pot. Cook fettuccine until just *al dente*. While fettucine is cooking, melt butter in a saucepan. Add salt, pepper, oregano and garlic and simmer together on very low heat. Sprinkle drained fettuccine with cheese. Pour butter sauce over all and serve.

## Baked Fillet of Flounder

½ teaspoon pepper
  Salt to taste
¼ teaspoon oregano
1 cup dry bread crumbs
½ cup grated Romano cheese
4 sprigs parsley, minced
1 clove garlic, minced
2 eggs
1½ pounds fillet of flounder
1 cup oil
  Butter
  Lemon slices

Mix pepper, salt, oregano, bread crumbs, cheese, parsley and garlic. Beat eggs. Dip fillets into eggs, then into bread crumb mixture. Heat oil in skillet. Fry fillets until golden brown on both sides. Place in buttered baking dish, dot with butter and lay lemon slices on top. Bake in a 350° oven for 10 minutes. Serve hot.

## Bibb Lettuce Salad with Grapes

3 heads Bibb lettuce
1 pound green or red grapes, washed
  Pinch of salt
¼ teaspoon pepper
⅛ teaspoon oregano
1 clove garlic, minced
5 tablespoons oil
1 tablespoon wine vinegar

Wash lettuce and pat leaves dry with paper towels. Break leaves into bite-size pieces and put in salad bowl. Gently toss with grapes. Add salt, pepper, oregano and garlic. Mix oil and vinegar and sprinkle over salad. Toss gently.

## Ricotta Pie

2 cups flour
½ teaspoon salt
1 cup lard
2 egg yolks
2 tablespoons cold water
3½ cups ricotta cheese
¼ cup flour
1 tablespoon grated orange peel
1 tablespoon grated lemon peel
1 tablespoon vanilla
½ teaspoon salt
1 teaspoon cinnamon
4 eggs
1 cup sugar

Grease a 9-inch pie pan. Mix 2 cups flour, ½ teaspoon salt and the lard. Add egg yolks and water. Blend until well mixed. Shape into ball and flatten on floured surface. Roll out pastry to a circle 1 inch larger than pie pan. Place in pan; pinch edge of pastry to stand up ¼ inch above pan.

Mix ricotta, ¼ cup flour, the orange and lemon peels, vanilla, ½ teaspoon salt and the cinnamon. Beat eggs until light and foamy. Stir eggs into ricotta mixture. Add sugar gradually, a little at a time. Pour into pie pan. Bake in a preheated 350° oven until mixture is firm, about 1 hour. Cool before serving.

66 Few people know what to do with ricotta cheese, but it's very versatile. Use it in lasagne, manicotti, cannoli, puddings and pies. It's much creamier tasting than cottage cheese. It used to be hard to find ricotta cheese, but many of the big grocery chain stores are carrying it now. 99

# Scampi!

**FRIED SHRIMP WITH
GARLIC SAUCE**

**SAUTEED ZUCCHINI**

**FRENCH FRIED ONION RINGS**

**CAULIFLOWER SALAD**

**BREAD AND BUTTER**

**ZABAGLIONE**

*

**SERVES 4**

## Fried Shrimp with Garlic Sauce

    2 pounds shrimp
    1 teaspoon salt
    ½ teaspoon pepper
    ⅛ teaspoon oregano
    1 clove garlic, minced
    ¼ cup grated Parmesan cheese
    1½ cups bread crumbs
    2 eggs
    ¼ cup milk
      Oil for frying
      Garlic Sauce (below)

Cook shrimp in boiling salted water until pink. Peel and devein shrimp. Rinse in cold water and drain on paper towels. Mix together salt, pepper, oregano, garlic, cheese and bread crumbs. Beat eggs and milk. Dip shrimp in egg mixture, then in seasoned bread crumbs. Heat oil in deep skillet and fry shrimp until golden brown. Pour Garlic Sauce over the shrimp; serve immediately.

### Garlic Sauce

    2 cloves garlic, minced
    1 teaspoon salt
    ¼ teaspoon oregano
    ¼ teaspoon pepper
    2 sprigs parsley, chopped
    ¼ cup oil

Cook garlic, salt, oregano, pepper and parsley in oil until the garlic is light brown.

## Sautéed Zucchini

    4 medium zucchini
    3 tablespoons oil
    1 clove garlic, minced
    3 tablespoons wine vinegar
    3 tablespoons water
    3 anchovies
      Salt to taste
    ⅛ teaspoon pepper
      Grated Parmesan cheese

Cut off ends of zucchini and slice ⅛ inch thick. Heat oil in a skillet. Add garlic and sauté until golden brown. Add zucchini and cover pan for a few minutes. Add vinegar, water and anchovies. Simmer for 10 to 15 minutes. Add salt and pepper, sprinkle with cheese and serve.

## French Fried Onion Rings

2 large onions
2 cups milk
2 eggs
1 teaspoon salt
¼ teaspoon pepper
⅛ teaspoon oregano
1 clove garlic, minced
2 sprigs parsley, chopped
1 cup flour
  Oil for deep frying

Slice onions crosswise into ¼-inch slices. Separate rings. Soak onions in milk for 20 minutes. Drain on paper towels. Beat eggs, salt, pepper, oregano, garlic and parsley in a flat dish. First dip onion rings in egg mixture, then in flour. Deep fry in oil, a few at a time, until golden brown.

## Cauliflower Salad

1 small head cauliflower
2 small potatoes, boiled, peeled and diced
  Pinch of salt
¼ teaspoon pepper
⅛ teaspoon oregano
1 clove garlic, minced
¼ cup oil
1 tablespoon wine vinegar
2 tablespoons grated Romano cheese

Wash cauliflower; separate into flowerets. Cook in boiling water about 10 minutes, until tender (not mushy). Drain; put into salad bowl. Add potatoes, salt, pepper, oregano and garlic. Mix oil and vinegar; sprinkle over salad. Toss gently; sprinkle with cheese.

## Zabaglione

4 egg yolks, beaten
¼ cup sugar
½ cup Marsala wine
1 teaspoon vanilla

Place egg yolks, sugar and Marsala in top of a double boiler and beat until well blended. Holding pan over boiling water (don't let it touch the water), beat until thick, fluffy and light. Blend in vanilla. Serve hot or cold, in dessert glasses.

66 Cooks are not born. They're made. When I was a young bride, I moved to Chicago. In my husband's family there were so many excellent cooks that I was actually ashamed to go ask my sisters-in-law to help me. Every day I'd go to a different person I knew so they wouldn't think I was *that* dumb. I'd say, "What are you cooking today?" And they'd say, "Oh, I'm having zucchini." "Well," I'd say, "tell me. I'd like some. What do I do?" And that was the way I learned to cook. Who'd ever know that so many years later, I'd have a restaurant and make use of all these little things those ladies taught me? 99

# Elegant But Easy

SPAGHETTI WITH SHRIMP
WATERCRESS SALAD
BREAD AND BUTTER
PEARS STUFFED WITH
GORGONZOLA CHEESE

*

SERVES 4

## Spaghetti with Shrimp

1 pound fresh shrimp
2 cloves garlic, minced
2 small onions, chopped
1 green pepper, chopped
  Salt
¼ teaspoon pepper
⅛ teaspoon oregano
¼ cup oil
6 quarts water
1 pound spaghetti
¼ cup grated Romano cheese

Boil shrimp until barely tender. Shell and devein shrimp. Sauté garlic, onions, green pepper, pinch of salt, pepper and oregano in oil until onions are soft. Add cooked shrimp. Stir and cook over low heat for 10 minutes.

Bring water and 1 tablespoon salt to rolling boil in a large pot; add spaghetti and cook until *al dente*. Drain in colander. Toss gently with shrimp mixture. Sprinkle with cheese and serve.

## Watercress Salad

1 large bunch watercress
2 small onions, diced
¼ cup oil
1 tablespoon wine vinegar
¼ teaspoon pepper
1 (2-ounce) can anchovies, drained
1 (2-ounce) bottle capers, drained
2 cloves garlic, minced
  Grated Romano cheese

Trim stem ends of watercress; wash and pat dry with paper towels. Mix together all ingredients except cheese and toss gently. Sprinkle with a little cheese.

## Pears Stuffed with Gorgonzola Cheese

4 fresh pears, peeled, halved and cored
  Lemon juice
3 ounces Gorgonzola cheese
3 tablespoons butter
3 tablespoons finely crushed nuts
  Lettuce leaves

Dip pears in lemon juice to keep them from turning brown. Cream Gorgonzola cheese and butter until smooth and fluffy. Fill centers of 4 pear halves with the creamed mixture; then press together with remaining halves to form whole pears. Roll in nuts and arrange on plate with lettuce leaves. Chill for 1 hour.

32

Spaghetti with Shrimp (page 32)

Italian Salad Regis (page 33)

## Tripe with Potatoes

1½ pounds tripe, cut into strips
¼ cup olive oil
2 onions, chopped
2 cloves garlic, minced
3 sprigs parsley, chopped
1 bay leaf
　 Pinch of salt
¼ teaspoon pepper
¼ teaspoon dried red pepper
　 flakes
1 (29-ounce) can plum
　 tomatoes, crushed
4 red potatoes, peeled and
　 cubed

Wash tripe in cold water. Cook slowly in lightly salted water for 2 hours or until nearly tender; drain. Heat oil in a saucepan and brown tripe, onions and garlic. Add all other ingredients and simmer slowly, covered, for 1 hour. Add more salt if necessary.

## Boiled Mustard Greens

2 pounds fresh mustard greens
2 cloves garlic, minced
¼ cup olive oil
　 Pinch of salt
½ teaspoon pepper

Remove wilted leaves and roots from mustard greens; wash greens well. Cook in boiling salted water for 10 minutes; drain. Brown garlic in oil. Add mustard greens, salt and pepper. Cook for a few minutes, then serve.

## Italian Salad Regis

3 tablespoons oil
1 tablespoon wine vinegar
1 head lettuce, torn into pieces
6 thin slices of your favorite
　 cheese, cut up
6 thin slices ham, cut up
6 thin slices roast beef, cut up
1 green pepper, chopped
18 thin slices pepperoni
1 onion, finely chopped
1 clove garlic, minced
　 Salt to taste
⅛ teaspoon oregano
1 tablespoon grated Romano
　 cheese
2 or 3 tomatoes, cut into wedges

Shake oil and vinegar together. Put all other ingredients except Romano cheese and tomatoes in a salad bowl and toss gently. Drizzle oil and vinegar over salad. Sprinkle with Romano cheese. Garnish with tomato wedges.

# A Hearty Boiled Dinner

**TRIPE WITH POTATOES**
**BOILED MUSTARD GREENS**
**ITALIAN SALAD REGIS**
**LEMON ICE (PAGE 53)**

*

**SERVES 4**

33

# Homemade Ravioli

RAVIOLI
CABBAGE AND
GREEN BEAN SALAD
BREAD AND BUTTER
FRESH FRUIT
MAMA D'S FILLED COOKIES

*

SERVES 6

### Ravioli

¾  pound ground beef
¾  pound ricotta cheese
3  eggs, beaten
1  cup grated Parmesan cheese
   Pinch of nutmeg
   Salt and pepper to taste
6  quarts water
1  tablespoon salt
   Ravioli Dough (right)
   Spaghetti sauce of your
   choice
   Grated Parmesan cheese

Mix ground beef, ricotta, eggs, 1 cup Parmesan cheese, the nutmeg and salt and pepper to taste together in a bowl; set aside. Make Ravioli Dough.

Bring 6 quarts water and 1 tablespoon salt to a rolling boil in a large pot. Add ravioli and cook until tender. Drain in a colander. Before serving, pour hot spaghetti sauce over the ravioli and sprinkle with additional grated Parmesan cheese.

### *Ravioli Dough*

3  cups flour
3  eggs, beaten
1  tablespoon oil
1  scant tablespoon salt
   Water

Place flour in a bowl. Make a well in the center and drop in eggs, oil and salt. Add water a little at a time (enough to make a smooth dough) and knead on a floured board until the dough is smooth and elastic. Invert a large bowl over the dough and let sit for 5 minutes. Divide the dough into 5 sections and roll out each section into a very thin rectangle. Cut the rectangles into strips, about 3x10 inches. Drop 1 teaspoon of filling on a strip at 2-inch intervals. Mold another strip of dough on top and cut with a ravioli cutter into 2x2-inch squares. (Or cut with a knife; press edges with a fork to seal.) Place ravioli on a lightly floured board and cover with a clean cloth.

## Cabbage and Green Bean Salad

½ head cabbage, shredded
1 (29-ounce) can French-cut green beans, drained
3 small carrots, shredded
2 onions, finely diced
1 green pepper, finely diced
2 stalks celery, cut up
3 sprigs parsley, chopped
2 cloves garlic, minced
   Pinch of salt
½ teaspoon pepper
⅛ teaspoon oregano
5 tablespoons oil
1 tablespoon wine vinegar
1 tomato, cut into wedges

Mix cabbage, beans, carrots, onions, green pepper, celery, parsley and garlic in a bowl. Season with salt, pepper and oregano. Mix oil and vinegar together, pour over salad and toss gently. Garnish with tomato wedges.

## Mama D's Filled Cookies

1 (6-ounce) jar peach preserves
1 (4-ounce) jar orange marmalade
1 cup chopped walnuts
1 cup white raisins
1 teaspoon cinnamon
¾ cup vegetable shortening
1½ cups granulated sugar
6 eggs, beaten
2 tablespoons vanilla
2 tablespoons baking powder
3 to 4 cups flour
   Confectioners' sugar

Mix preserves, marmalade, nuts, raisins and cinnamon; set aside.

Cream shortening and granulated sugar. Add eggs and blend thoroughly. Mix in vanilla, baking powder and 3 cups of the flour. Gradually add more flour until dough reaches the consistency of pie crust. Mix well. Knead until dough is smooth.

Roll out dough to about ¼-inch thickness on lightly floured board. Cut into 3x10-inch strips. On lower half of each pastry strip, drop 1 teaspoon filling at 2-inch intervals. Fold over the top half and cut into individual cookies with a round glass or cutter. Press edges with a fork to seal. Place cookies on a greased cookie sheet and bake in a preheated 375° oven for 10 to 15 minutes, until golden brown. Sprinkle with confectioners' sugar. Makes 6 to 8 dozen cookies.

66 Fresh food is still the best. I never buy frozen meat, because it doesn't appeal to me. We should go back to eating more hearty foods. Some of the food placed in front of kids today is nothing to come home to, believe me. Don't just throw a TV dinner in front of your family. Think of something to cook. It doesn't take long to boil a potato and cook some vegetables and meat. 99

# For Very Special Guests

MARINATED STEAK
CAPONATINA EGGPLANT
ESCAROLE SALAD
BREAD AND BUTTER
HONEY CLUSTERS
*
SERVES 4 TO 6

## Marinated Steak

3-pound T-bone steak
1 cup oil
¼ cup wine vinegar
4 sprigs parsley, chopped
2 cloves garlic, minced
¼ teaspoon oregano
¼ teaspoon pepper
Mushrooms and Onions
(below)

Place steak in a shallow baking dish. Mix oil, vinegar, parsley, garlic, oregano and pepper and pour over steak. Marinate steak for at least 3 or 4 hours, turning often. Remove steak. Pat dry with paper towels and broil 3 inches from heat for 5 minutes on each side, or to your own taste. Cover steak with Mushrooms and Onions and serve.

### Mushrooms and Onions

1 pound fresh mushrooms
¼ cup oil
2 onions, chopped
Salt and pepper to taste

Sauté mushrooms in oil; add onions and simmer slowly until onions are transparent. Add salt and pepper.

## Caponatina Eggplant

2 small eggplants
Salt
¼ cup olive oil
1 small stalk celery, chopped
(use leaves, too)
2 small onions, chopped
½ cup vinegar
5 teaspoons sugar
1 (29-ounce) can plum tomatoes, drained
10 green olives, pitted and slivered
1 (3½-ounce) bottle capers, drained
1 (2-ounce) can anchovies
1 teaspoon salt
¼ teaspoon pepper

Pare eggplants and cut into ½-inch cubes. Salt generously and drain in colander. Heat olive oil in large skillet. Add chopped celery. Cook for 10 minutes. Add onions and sauté until soft and light colored. Transfer celery and onions to a bowl with a slotted spoon. Sauté eggplant about 10 minutes in remaining oil until lightly browned. Mix vinegar and sugar. Return the celery and onions to skillet and stir in the vinegar and sugar, tomatoes, olives, capers, anchovies, 1 teaspoon salt and the pepper. Bring to a boil, reduce heat and simmer, uncovered, for 20 minutes. Taste for salt and pepper. If necessary, add a little more vinegar. Simmer a few more minutes and put in a serving bowl. Refrigerate.

36

## Escarole Salad

1  head escarole
1  small onion, minced
1  teaspoon salt
¼  teaspoon pepper
1  clove garlic, minced
⅛  teaspoon oregano
¼  cup oil
1  tablespoon vinegar

Wash escarole and tear into pieces. Add minced onion. Season with salt, pepper, garlic and oregano. Mix oil and vinegar. Drizzle over salad and toss very lightly.

## Honey Clusters

2  cups sifted flour
¼  teaspoon salt
3  eggs
1  teaspoon vanilla
   Oil for frying
½  cup honey
½  cup sugar
   Multicolor candy sprinkles

Put flour and salt in a bowl. Make a well and add the eggs one at a time. Beat well after adding each egg; add vanilla and mix until you get a soft dough. Knead on a lightly floured surface, divide dough and roll out to ¼-inch thickness. Cut strips ¼ inch wide. Use palms of hands to roll strips to the thickness of pencils. Cut ½ inch long. Fry in hot oil in skillet, one layer deep (do not crowd); turn. Remove when golden on all sides.

Heat honey and sugar in skillet for 5 minutes over medium heat. Remove from heat and add deep-fried pieces. Stir until honey mixture covers all pieces. Remove with a slotted spoon and let cool. Decorate with sprinkles; break off and serve in pieces.

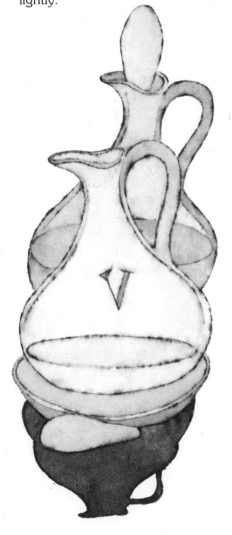

66 If you're entertaining friends, you'd better serve good coffee because that makes the meal. If your food is good and your coffee is bad, your whole meal is spoiled. When you buy cheap coffee, it has to have something cheap added to it. At our restaurant we pay a little more for our coffee, but people say it's exceptionally good. 99

# Celebrating March 19

BARBECUED CHICKEN

RICE BALLS

MIXED SALAD

BREAD AND BUTTER

ST. JOSEPH'S DAY
SWEET RAVIOLI

*

SERVES 4

## Barbecued Chicken

3- to 3½-pound chicken
½ cup oil
  Salt to taste
5 sprigs parsley, chopped
2 cloves garlic, minced
½ teaspoon pepper
¼ teaspoon oregano
½ teaspoon paprika
  Barbecue Sauce (below)

Cut chicken into serving pieces. Grease a cookie sheet with sides or a shallow baking dish. Put chicken in a bowl and add oil, salt, parsley, garlic, pepper and oregano. Toss together gently. Place on a greased cookie sheet and sprinkle with paprika. Bake in a 375° oven for about 1 hour, or until tender. Pour Barbecue Sauce over chicken; lower heat to 350° and cook chicken for 10 more minutes.

## Barbecue Sauce

2 onions, chopped
1 clove garlic, minced
¼ cup oil
1 (29-ounce) can tomato puree
¼ cup vinegar
2 tablespoons brown sugar
½ cup catsup
½ teaspoon marjoram
½ teaspoon dry mustard

Brown onion and garlic in oil. Add tomato puree, vinegar, brown sugar, catsup, marjoram and mustard and simmer for 1½ hours.

## Rice Balls

2 cups cooked rice
3 eggs, beaten
¼ cup flour
½ cup grated Romano cheese
  Salt
¼ teaspoon oregano
½ teaspoon pepper
1 clove garlic, minced
2 sprigs parsley, chopped
1 cup dry bread crumbs
½ cup grated Romano cheese
¼ teaspoon oregano
½ teaspoon pepper
2 cloves garlic, minced
  Oil for frying

Mix together rice, eggs, flour, ½ cup cheese, salt to taste, ¼ teaspoon oregano, ½ teaspoon pepper, 1 clove garlic, minced, and the parsley. Taste for seasoning.

Mix remaining ingredients except oil. Roll rice mixture into small balls, about 1¼ inches in diameter. Dip in seasoned bread crumbs. Heat about 1½ inches of oil in an 8- or 10-inch skillet. Fry rice balls about 2 minutes on each side, until golden brown.

## Mixed Salad

Select any vegetables you would like to use (cucumbers, celery, radishes, onions, chick-peas, tomatoes, lettuce, escarole, green peppers, etc.). Tear lettuce into bite-size pieces; place in a bowl. Chop other ingredients and add to bowl. Season to taste with salt, pepper, oregano and minced garlic. Drizzle with oil and wine vinegar dressing (4 parts oil to 1 part vinegar).

## St. Joseph's Day Sweet Ravioli

2 cups ricotta cheese
Sugar to taste
1 teaspoon cinnamon
2 eggs, beaten
Ravioli Dough (page 34)
Oil for deep frying
Confectioners' sugar

Mix ricotta, sugar, cinnamon and eggs very thoroughly; set aside.

Follow the basic instructions for preparing Ravioli Dough, using ricotta mixture for the filling. Deep fry in hot oil. Drain on paper towels and sprinkle with confectioners' sugar.

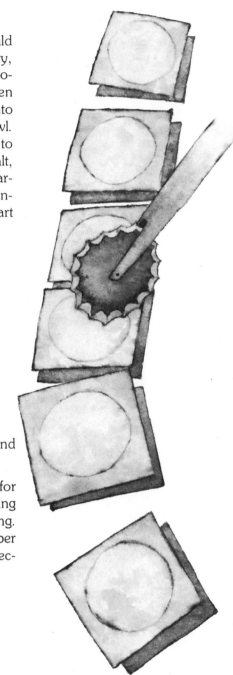

66 When you're making salads, *drip* the oil on. Don't *pour* it or it will just run into the bottom of the bowl and what good is that? If you're using tomatoes in your salad, you don't really need vinegar. The tomato has enough acid, and all you need is the oil with the herbs. Always season your lettuce with the herbs before you add the oil. When you add the herbs to the salad dressing, the oil coats the spices and you don't get all of the flavor. For a really flavorful salad, put the seasonings on the lettuce and let the lettuce stand in the refrigerator for 2 or 3 hours before serving. 99

39

# For a Chilly Evening

**POT ROAST
WITH VEGETABLES**

**SPINACH AND CURLY ENDIVE
SALAD**

**BREAD AND BUTTER**

**FRUIT MACEDONIA**

*

**SERVES 6**

## Pot Roast with Vegetables

4- to 4½-pound pot roast
  Salt to taste
  Pepper
  Oregano
2  cloves garlic, minced
4  sprigs parsley, chopped
¼  cup flour
½  cup oil
5  carrots, scraped and
   quartered
4  potatoes, peeled and
   quartered
2  small onions, sliced and
   separated into rings
2  tablespoons grated Romano
   cheese
½  cup dry red wine

Season pot roast with salt, pepper and oregano to taste. Make slits in roast with sharp knife. Put a little more salt, pepper and oregano, along with the garlic and parsley, in each slit. Coat roast with flour.

Heat oil in large skillet, brown roast on all sides and put in roasting pan. Place carrots and potatoes next to pot roast and arrange onion rings on top. Sprinkle with cheese. Add wine and bake, covered, in a 350° oven for about 4 hours or until meat is tender.

## Spinach and Curly Endive Salad

1  pound fresh spinach, washed
1  bunch curly endive
   Salt to taste
½  teaspoon pepper
¼  teaspoon oregano
¼  cup oil
1  tablespoon wine vinegar

Crisp spinach in ice water and drain well. Cut up endive and spinach leaves and put in a salad bowl. Sprinkle with salt, pepper and oregano. Mix oil and vinegar and pour over all. Toss gently.

## Fruit Macedonia

Select fresh or canned fruits of your choice—as many varieties as you wish (bananas, apples, melons, oranges, peaches, etc.). Cut into small pieces. Pour ½ cup cherry or fruit brandy over all. Chill for at least 1 hour. Serve in sherbet glasses.

## Polenta with Sausage

3 tablespoons oil
1 pound Italian sausages, cut up
2 small onions, sliced
1 pound fresh mushrooms, sliced, or 2 (8-ounce) cans sliced mushrooms, drained
  Salt
¼ teaspoon pepper
⅛ teaspoon oregano
2 cloves garlic, minced
1 (29-ounce) can tomatoes, crushed
4 cups water
1½ cups cornmeal
¼ cup grated Romano cheese

Heat oil in a skillet. Brown sausages and onions. Add mushrooms, a pinch of salt, the pepper, oregano and garlic. Sauté for 5 minutes. Add tomatoes; simmer slowly for 1 hour. Bring the water and a pinch of salt to a boil in a saucepan. Stir in cornmeal and continue boiling until thick. (Keep stirring the mixture so it doesn't burn.) Cover, lower heat and cook slowly, stirring frequently, for 5 to 10 minutes. (Total cooking time should be 20 to 30 minutes.) Transfer cornmeal to a warm platter; spread on the sausage-mushroom mixture. Sprinkle with cheese.

## Green Beans with Tomatoes

3 tablespoons oil
1 onion, finely chopped
2 cloves garlic, minced
1 (20-ounce) can tomatoes, crushed
1½ pounds fresh green beans, cooked, or 1 (29-ounce) can green beans, drained
  Pinch of salt
½ teaspoon pepper
⅛ teaspoon oregano
¼ cup grated Parmesan cheese

Heat oil in a skillet. Brown onion and garlic. Add tomatoes, green beans, salt, pepper and oregano. Simmer slowly for 25 minutes. Sprinkle with cheese and serve.

## Frozen Peaches

2 cups water
2 cups sugar
2 tablespoons Marsala wine
6 canned peach halves
1 cup whipping cream, whipped
6 maraschino cherries

Mix water, sugar and Marsala together; stir until sugar is dissolved. Pour this mixture into a refrigerator tray. Arrange peach halves, cut side up, in the tray and freeze. Cut into squares. Top with whipped cream and garnish each square with a maraschino cherry.

# A Northern Italian Favorite

**POLENTA WITH SAUSAGE**

**GREEN BEANS WITH TOMATOES**

**MIXED SALAD (PAGE 39)**

**BREAD AND BUTTER**

**FROZEN PEACHES**

*

**SERVES 4 TO 6**

# Sage
# Makes It
# Special

**LENTIL SOUP**

**SALTIMBOCCA**

**TOMATOES STUFFED WITH MUSHROOMS**

**BREAD AND BUTTER**

**ITALIAN RUM CAKE**

\*

**SERVES 4**

## Lentil Soup

1 pound dried lentils
5 quarts water
2 cloves garlic, minced
4 to 6 potatoes, peeled and diced
¼ cup oil
4 onions, diced
½ teaspoon pepper
  Salt to taste
1½ cups plum tomatoes, chopped
4 carrots, diced
3 tablespoons butter

Wash lentils and soak in water overnight; drain. Bring 5 quarts fresh water to a boil and add all ingredients. Cook slowly for 2½ hours. Taste; add more seasonings if necessary.

## Saltimbocca

¼ cup oil
1 tablespoon butter
8 thin slices veal (cut from the leg or shoulder), pounded
  Pinch of salt
½ teaspoon pepper
¼ teaspoon oregano
  Sage
1 clove garlic, minced
8 slices prosciutto ham
¼ cup grated mozzarella cheese
½ cup white wine
1 (4-ounce) can whole mushrooms

Heat oil and butter in skillet. Brown veal lightly on both sides. Remove from pan. Season veal with salt, pepper, oregano, sage (to taste) and garlic. Put a slice of prosciutto ham on each slice of veal. Sprinkle with mozzarella cheese. Roll veal slices and filling up and fasten with toothpicks. Return to skillet and add wine and mushrooms. Simmer slowly until most of liquid evaporates. Serve immediately.

## Tomatoes Stuffed with Mushrooms

4 large tomatoes
¼ cup olive oil
2 tablespoons butter
1 onion, finely chopped
1 clove garlic, minced
1 (2-ounce) can sliced mushrooms
4 chicken livers, finely chopped
Pinch of salt
¼ teaspoon pepper
⅛ teaspoon oregano
1 cup bread crumbs
2 tablespoons grated Romano cheese
2 eggs, beaten
1 hard-cooked egg, chopped
Oil

Wash tomatoes and cut off thin slice from stem end of each. Scoop out pulp and seeds. Heat olive oil and butter together in a saucepan and sauté onion and garlic. Add mushrooms and livers. Stir and cook for 7 minutes. Remove from heat. Add remaining ingredients except oil and mix. Stuff tomatoes. Grease a baking sheet. Set tomatoes upright on baking sheet and brush with oil. Bake in a 350° oven 30 minutes.

## Italian Rum Cake

6 eggs, separated
½ cup granulated sugar
1 tablespoon lemon juice
1 tablespoon orange juice
2 teaspoons rum extract
1 cup cake flour
Pinch of salt
Confectioners' sugar

Preheat oven to 350°. Beat egg yolks until thick. Beat in granulated sugar, the lemon and orange juice and rum extract. Sift flour twice; add flour gradually to egg yolk mixture. Beat egg whites until foamy. Add salt and beat until stiff. Fold into egg yolk mixture. Pour batter into springform pan. Bake for 1 hour. Cool cake in pan. Invert on rack and remove from pan. When cake is cool, sprinkle it with confectioners' sugar.

66 I'd be a poor ad for canned or purchased soups. Making soup costs so little. You can serve the same soup so many different ways with a little ingenuity. Serve soup two or three times a week during the winter. It's good for children, and they love it. Canned soups may be enriched with things like vitamins, but they also have chemical additives or they wouldn't be able to stay on the shelf unrefrigerated for so long. 99

# Snails for Supper

**SNAILS WITH GARLIC BUTTER SAUCE OR TOMATO SAUCE**

**LINGUINE**

**ANTIPASTO SALAD**

**FRESH FRUIT**

*

**SERVES 4 TO 6**

## Snails

2  pounds live snails
   Water
3  tablespoons salt
   Garlic Butter Sauce or Tomato Sauce (right)

Put snails in a large pot. Cover with water and 2 tablespoons salt. Let stand for 3 hours. Keep covered because snails will creep up. Rinse many times in fresh water and drain. Cover snails with fresh water to 2 inches from top of pot. Add 1 tablespoon salt. Cover and cook over low heat until snails start to protrude from shells. Turn heat up to medium and cook for 45 minutes. Remove from heat, cool about 10 minutes and drain; or drain and run cool water over snails, then drain again. Serve with either Garlic Butter Sauce or Tomato Sauce.

## Garlic Butter Sauce

1½  cups (¾ pound) butter
2   cloves garlic, minced
    Salt and pepper to taste
¼   teaspoon oregano

Melt butter in a saucepan. Add garlic, salt, pepper and oregano; simmer over low heat until garlic is lightly browned. Return drained snails to their cooking pot. Pour sauce over snails and stir until butter and snails are mixed well. Serve in shells. Use a small oyster fork or nut pick to extract the meat. Drink butter from the shells.

## Tomato Sauce

2   cloves garlic, minced
1   small onion, chopped
¼   cup oil
2   (29-ounce) cans Italian tomatoes, crushed
1   (6-ounce) can tomato paste
2   (6-ounce) cans water
    Pinch of salt
½   teaspoon pepper
⅛   teaspoon oregano

Brown garlic and onion in hot oil until lightly browned. Add tomatoes, tomato paste, water, salt, pepper and oregano and stir until well blended. Cook for 1 hour over low heat. Add cooked snails and simmer slowly for 20 minutes. Remove snails to individual bowls with a slotted spoon. Serve remaining sauce over linguine.

## Linguine

6 quarts water
1 tablespoon salt
1 pound linguine
  Grated Parmesan cheese

Bring water and salt to rolling boil in large pot. Add linguine and cook until tender, about 15 minutes; drain in colander. Pour snail sauce over linguine. (If you're serving Snails with Garlic Butter Sauce, serve linguine as an accompaniment.) Sprinkle with cheese.

## Antipasto Salad

4 slices cooked ham, diced
4 slices Swiss cheese, diced
6 slices roast beef, diced
¼ pound sausage, cooked and diced
1 head lettuce, broken into chunks
  Salt, pepper, oregano and minced garlic to taste
3 teaspoons grated Parmesan cheese
2 tablespoons oil
1 tablespoon wine vinegar
1 tomato, cut into wedges

Combine ham, Swiss cheese, roast beef, sausage and lettuce chunks in a salad bowl. Sprinkle on salt, pepper, oregano, garlic and Parmesan cheese. Put oil and vinegar into a small jar and shake well. Drizzle over salad and toss. Garnish with tomato wedges.

66 Buy your Parmesan cheese in chunks and grate it yourself. You never know how long ago the grated cheese in containers was packed. Often it's dry and all the flavor is gone. Grate your cheese as you need it. Wrap the chunk of cheese in a wet cloth and keep it in your refrigerator. 99

# Chicken "Hunter's Style"

CHICKEN SOUP

CHICKEN CACCIATORE

SPICY POTATOES

TOMATO, ONION AND PEPPER SALAD

HOMEMADE ROLLS

SPUMONI ICE CREAM (PAGE 57)

*

SERVES 4

## Chicken Soup

Chicken back, neck, wing tips and giblets (left over from Cacciatore recipe, right)
2 sliced tomatoes or about ½ cup canned tomatoes
2 stalks celery, cut into pieces (use leaves, too)
2 carrots, sliced
1 bay leaf
Sprig of parsley
Salt and pepper to taste

Place all ingredients in a 3-quart pot, cover with water and bring to a boil. Lower heat and simmer soup, uncovered, for about 2 hours. Remove chicken and pick meat from bones; return meat to soup.

Serve hot, as is, or add a little cooked rice, small pasta shells or macaroni if desired.

## Chicken Cacciatore

½ cup oil
1 onion, finely chopped
3 cloves garlic, minced
Chopped fresh parsley or dried parsley to taste
Salt and pepper
Pinch of oregano
1 (29-ounce) can tomato puree
1 cup sweet red wine (not a dry wine—a Concord grape wine)
3½- to 4-pound chicken, cut into serving pieces (use back, neck, wing tips and giblets in Chicken Soup)
Oil
Oregano, garlic and dried parsley to taste
Paprika
Grated Parmesan cheese

Heat ½ cup oil in a 2-quart saucepan. Add onion, garlic, parsley, salt, pepper and pinch of oregano and sauté slowly until golden brown. Add tomato puree and wine and bring to a boil. Simmer slowly, uncovered, for about 1½ hours. After sauce has simmered for 30 minutes, prepare chicken.

Grease a baking pan. Place the chicken pieces in it, skin side up; brush generously with oil. Season with salt, pepper, oregano (sparingly), garlic and dried parsley. Sprinkle a little paprika over each piece of chicken. Bake in a 375° oven about 55 minutes, until tender and golden. Sprinkle with cheese, pour on sauce and serve.

### Spicy Potatoes

2  (16-ounce) cans small whole
   potatoes, drained
¼  cup oil
   Salt and pepper to taste
1  tablespoon chopped fresh
   parsley
   Pinch of oregano
2  cloves garlic, minced
2  tablespoons grated Parmesan
   cheese

Place potatoes in an ungreased
baking pan. Mix remaining ingredients and pour over potatoes.
Bake in a 375° oven for about 1
hour, turning several times, until
potatoes are golden brown all
over.

### Tomato, Onion and Pepper Salad

2  large tomatoes, sliced
1  large onion, sliced and
   separated into rings
1  large green pepper, seeded
   and sliced
1  teaspoon basil
   Salt and pepper to taste
   Pinch of oregano
1  clove garlic, minced
2  tablespoons grated Parmesan
   cheese
¼  cup oil

Place tomato slices on a platter.
Arrange onion rings on top. Garnish with green pepper slices.
Sprinkle with basil, salt, pepper,
oregano, garlic and cheese. Pour
oil slowly over all.

66 Before you cook fowl, rub
salt in the cavity and on the
outside. Then rinse the bird with
water.

Use fresh tomatoes if you can
find good ones. If you're cooking
with canned tomatoes, use any
Italian or plum tomatoes—
canned American tomatoes are
packed with too much water and
are more discolored. 99

# Warm Soup, Wonderful Soup

**VEGETABLE BEEF BONE SOUP**

**SAUTEED VEAL KIDNEYS**

**ITALIAN MIXED SALAD
(PAGE 51)**

**BREAD AND BUTTER**

**FRUIT AND FONTINA**

*

**SERVES 4**

## Vegetable Beef Bone Soup

1  large soup bone (or several
   small ones)
6  quarts water
   Salt to taste
3  carrots, sliced
3  stalks celery, sliced
2  potatoes, diced
2  onions, chopped
3  sprigs parsley
1  bay leaf
3  or 4 ripe tomatoes or 1
   (16-ounce) can tomatoes

Put soup bone and water in a large pot and add salt. When water comes to a boil, add carrots, celery, potatoes, onions, parsley, bay leaf and tomatoes. Simmer slowly for at least 2½ to 3 hours. Makes 12 servings.

Note: Refrigerate leftover soup for use the next day.

## Sautéed Veal Kidneys

3  veal kidneys
1  cup water
1  cup vinegar
1  bay leaf
6  tablespoons oil
2  cloves garlic, minced
3  sprigs parsley, chopped
¼  teaspoon pepper
   Salt to taste
2  tablespoons lemon juice

Peel membrane from kidneys and cut away all fat. Marinate kidneys for 30 minutes in mixture of water, vinegar and bay leaf. Drain kidneys and pat dry with paper towels. Discard liquid. Cut kidneys crosswise into thin slices. Heat oil in a skillet. Add kidney slices, garlic, parsley and pepper and cook gently for 3 to 4 minutes, until tender. Add salt and lemon juice and heat for 2 minutes longer. Serve on a heated platter.

## Fruit and Fontina

Serve fresh fruit (any fruit in season) arranged in a bowl; accompany with Fontina cheese.

Chicken Cacciatore (page 46)

Fruit and Fontina (page 48)

Lemon Ice (page 53)

Pizza (page 50)

Knead dough until smooth and soft—poke with your finger to test.

After dough has doubled in size, roll out to fit the pizza pan.

Spread tomato sauce on dough, then sprinkle with grated cheeses.

## Beef Scaloppine

2 pounds beef rump or
   tenderloin
   Pinch of salt
½ teaspoon pepper
2 cloves garlic, minced
¼ teaspoon oregano
1 cup flour
½ cup oil
½ cup white wine (dry or sweet)

Have your butcher slice the beef very thinly. Season beef slices with salt, pepper, garlic and oregano; coat with flour. Heat oil in skillet and brown beef slices for 1 or 2 minutes on each side—just until flour is golden brown. Leave beef in skillet and pour wine over it. Simmer, covered, for 5 minutes.

## Peas with Rice

¼ cup oil
2 small onions, diced
2 cloves garlic, minced
1 (29-ounce) can peas (fresh or
   frozen peas may also be used)
   Pinch of salt
½ teaspoon pepper
2 cups cooked rice
   Pinch of saffron
½ cup grated Romano cheese

Heat oil in saucepan; brown onions and garlic. Add peas, salt and pepper and simmer for 20 minutes. Add rice and saffron. Sprinkle with cheese and serve hot.

## Anchovy, Tomato and Lettuce Salad

1 head lettuce, torn into
   bite-size pieces
2 small tomatoes, cut into
   wedges
1 small onion, finely chopped
1 (2-ounce) can anchovies,
   drained and chopped
1 green pepper, sliced into
   lengthwise strips
10 stuffed green olives, sliced
   Salt to taste
½ teaspoon pepper
¼ teaspoon oregano
1 clove garlic, minced
¼ cup oil
1 tablespoon wine vinegar

Put lettuce, tomatoes, onion, anchovies, green pepper and olives into a salad bowl. Season with salt, pepper, oregano and garlic. Sprinkle with oil and vinegar and toss together gently.

# Offbeat Scaloppine

**BEEF SCALOPPINE**

**PEAS WITH RICE**

**ANCHOVY, TOMATO AND
LETTUCE SALAD**

**BREAD AND BUTTER**

**SESAME COOKIES (PAGE 53)**

\*

**SERVES 6**

# Mama D's Pizza Party

**PIZZA
SPAGHETTI WITH CLAM SAUCE
ITALIAN MIXED SALAD
PEACHES WITH MARSALA**

*

**SERVES 4 TO 6**

## Pizza

1  package dry yeast
    Warm water
4  cups flour
1  teaspoon salt
1  teaspoon sugar
½  cup oil
    Basic Tomato Sauce (right)
    Salt, pepper, oregano and
    minced garlic to taste
    Grated Parmesan cheese
    Grated mozzarella cheese

Dissolve yeast in 1 cup warm water. Mix the flour, salt and sugar in a bowl. Make a well and pour in the oil. Add yeast mixture and mix thoroughly. Knead the dough until it is soft and pliable. Add more warm water or flour to make it smooth, kneading well, until dough leaves the sides of the bowl. To test, press a finger into the dough. When indentation pops back, dough is ready. Place the bowl in a warm place and let the dough rise until doubled in size (about 1½ to 2 hours). Cover with a cloth until ready to roll out. (To make 2 small pizzas, divide dough into 2 balls.)

Preheat oven to 400°. Lightly grease a cookie sheet or large pizza pan. Roll out dough to the size of the pan(s), about ⅛ inch thick, and place on pan. Prick dough lightly all over with a fork. Spread Tomato Sauce on top. Season with salt, pepper, oregano and garlic. Sprinkle with cheeses. Bake for about 30 minutes, or until done.

## Basic Tomato Sauce

1  (29-ounce) can plum
    tomatoes in puree
1  large onion, chopped
¼  cup oil
    Salt, pepper, oregano and
    minced garlic to taste

Chop tomatoes finely or puree in a food mill. Sauté onion in oil; add salt, pepper, oregano, garlic and tomatoes. Simmer sauce for 15 minutes.

Note: For variety, you can add any or all of the following to your pizzas before baking: sliced mushrooms; sliced pepperoni; whole or chopped anchovies; chopped sweet pepper.

50

## Spaghetti with Clam Sauce

1 large onion, chopped
1 teaspoon chopped parsley
2 cloves garlic, minced
¼ cup oil
1 (7-ounce) can minced clams
   (undrained)
1 cup water
   Salt and pepper to taste
1 pound spaghetti
6 quarts water
1 tablespoon salt
   Grated Parmesan cheese

Sauté onion, parsley and garlic in oil until onion is golden brown. Add the clams, 1 cup water and salt and pepper to taste. Simmer for 1 hour.

Bring 6 quarts water and 1 tablespoon salt to rolling boil; cook spaghetti until *al dente*. Drain pasta and sprinkle with cheese. Pour clam sauce over pasta and serve immediately.

Note: You can use fettuccine instead of spaghetti if you like.

## Italian Mixed Salad

1 head lettuce, coarsely cut
1 small onion, finely chopped
½ cup chopped celery
1 cucumber, sliced
2 cloves garlic, minced
   Salt, pepper and oregano to
   taste
¼ cup oil
1 tablespoon vinegar
1 tomato, sliced or cut into
   wedges

Place lettuce, onion, celery and cucumber in a salad bowl. Add garlic, salt, pepper and oregano. Put oil and vinegar in a small bottle or jar and shake well. Pour over the salad and garnish with tomato.

## Peaches with Marsala

2 (16-ounce) cans peach halves,
   drained
   Marsala wine (¼ cup
   for each serving)

Arrange peach halves in sherbet glasses. Pour the wine over the peaches. Chill before serving.

Note: You can use fresh peaches, if they're in season; just peel them and cut in half. Allow 1 peach per person.

66 At the restaurant, I've made Italian-style breakfasts for people—Italian sausage browned and stirred into scrambled eggs seasoned with salt, pepper, oregano and garlic. I cut chunks of Italian bread—I don't like thin slices for breakfast—and toast them in the oven, not in a toaster.

Try crushing Italian tomatoes, heating them a little and stirring them into the eggs you are scrambling. Or, you can add a little spaghetti sauce. Vary "sunny side up" eggs by sprinkling them with salt, pepper, oregano, garlic and a little grated Parmesan or Romano cheese. 99

# Dinner in Milan

**BRAISED VEAL SHANKS**

**MILANESE RISOTTO**

**CUCUMBER, TOMATO AND ONION SALAD**

**LEMON ICE**

**SESAME COOKIES**

*

**SERVES 4 TO 6**

## Braised Veal Shanks

5  tablespoons butter
1  onion, finely chopped
2  carrots, finely chopped
2  stalks celery, finely chopped
2  cloves garlic, minced
4  to 8 veal shanks
    Flour
    Salt and pepper
½  cup oil
1  cup dry wine (white or red)
1  teaspoon basil
1  cup beef or chicken broth
1  (29-ounce) can tomato puree
2  teaspoons dried parsley
2  bay leaves

Melt butter in a Dutch oven or roasting pan. Add onion, carrots, celery and garlic. Sauté for 10 minutes; remove from heat. Rub veal shanks with flour and season with salt and pepper. Heat oil in skillet and brown shanks until golden brown, then place over vegetables in Dutch oven. Pour off oil from skillet; add wine to skillet and heat until it boils briskly. Stir in basil, broth, tomato puree, parsley and bay leaves. Bring to a boil and pour over veal shanks. If liquid doesn't cover the bottom half of the veal shanks, add more broth. Cover and bake in a 375° oven for 1½ hours or until the shanks are tender. Taste for salt and pepper.

## Milanese Risotto

6  cups chicken broth
2  onions, chopped
5  tablespoons butter
2  cups uncooked rice
⅔  cup dry wine (white or red)
4  tablespoons butter, softened
½  cup grated Parmesan cheese
⅛  teaspoon saffron

Bring chicken broth to a boil in a 4-quart saucepan. In a heavy casserole sauté chopped onions in 5 tablespoons butter until very light brown. Add the rice to the onions and cook, stirring, until the grains are coated with butter. Pour in the wine. Stir and cook for 5 minutes. Add broth, a little at a time. When all broth has been added and rice is soft, stir, then add 4 tablespoons butter, the cheese and saffron. Serve piping hot.

## Cucumber, Tomato and Onion Salad

8 radishes, sliced
1 cucumber, sliced
3 tomatoes, quartered
3 stalks celery, diced (use
   leaves, too)
   Salt to taste
¼ teaspoon pepper
⅛ teaspoon oregano
1 clove garlic, minced
2 onions, finely chopped
¼ cup oil
1 tablespoon wine vinegar

Mix all ingredients except oil and vinegar in a bowl. Shake the oil and vinegar together in a small jar and pour over the salad. Season to taste.

## Lemon Ice

2 cups water
1 cup sugar
1 cup lemon juice

In a 2-quart saucepan, bring water and sugar to a boil, stirring until the sugar dissolves. Boil mixture for 5 minutes. Remove from heat and cool. Stir in lemon juice. Pour into a refrigerator tray. Place in freezer for 4 hours, stirring occasionally, until mixture is the texture of snow.

## Sesame Cookies

3 cups flour
1 cup sugar
2 teaspoons baking powder
   Pinch of salt
1 cup shortening
3 eggs, beaten
¼ cup milk
1 cup sesame seeds

Mix flour, sugar, baking powder and salt. Cut shortening into dry mixture. Add beaten eggs and milk and mix well. Break off pieces and make 1½-inch rolls. Roll in sesame seeds. Place about ½ inch apart on a greased cookie sheet. Bake in a preheated 375° oven for about 20 minutes until light brown. Makes 6 to 8 dozen cookies.

❝ Hands are the best mixers in the world. They beat any electric mixer.

Cook with what you have. You don't need fancy special bowls and pans. It's nice if you have all the fancy gadgets—but you don't need them to be a good cook. Cooking for your family with love is the most important thing. ❞

# Seafood Supreme

LOBSTER FRA DIAVOLO
STUFFED ARTICHOKES
BROCCOLI SALAD
BREAD AND BUTTER
MACAROONS
*
SERVES 4

## Lobster Fra Diavolo

4 lobster tails, about 1 pound each (or use smaller ones)
¼ cup olive oil
2 cloves garlic, minced
1¼ teaspoons salt
¼ teaspoon pepper
⅛ teaspoon oregano
1 teaspoon dried parsley or 3 sprigs parsley, chopped
1 (29-ounce) can tomato puree
½ cup white or red wine
Few grains cayenne pepper

Cook lobster tails in boiling salted water until pink. Remove lobster from shells and keep warm. Place olive oil, garlic, salt, pepper, oregano, parsley and tomato puree in saucepan. Simmer for 45 minutes. Add wine and cayenne pepper; simmer for 15 minutes more. Pour over lobster meat.

Note: Leftover sauce may be used over spaghetti or rice.

## Stuffed Artichokes

4 medium artichokes
1 teaspoon salt
½ teaspoon pepper
2 or 3 sprigs parsley, chopped
¼ teaspoon oregano
1 clove garlic, minced
½ cup grated Parmesan cheese
½ cup bread crumbs
Water
¼ cup oil

Remove tough lower leaves from artichokes. Wash with salted water; shake off excess water. Mix salt, pepper, parsley, oregano, garlic, cheese and bread crumbs in bowl. Spread artichoke leaves, starting from outside, and stuff seasoned bread dressing in between until all layers of leaves have been filled. Place stuffed artichokes in a 6-quart pot. Add 2 inches of water, sprinkle with oil, place over medium heat and cover. Cook for 20 minutes. Baste with water and oil mixture. Add more water if necessary. Lower heat to a simmer and cook another 40 minutes, until done. Serve as is or add more salt and pepper.

## Broccoli Salad

1   head broccoli
    Salt and pepper to taste
1   clove garlic, minced
¼   cup oil
    Grated Parmesan cheese
    Lemon wedges

Cut off and discard tough end of broccoli head. Separate into flowerets and peel stems. Wash in cold water. Cook broccoli in boiling salted water until tender; drain. Place on platter and season with salt, pepper and garlic. Sprinkle with oil and cheese. Serve with lemon wedges. May be served hot or cold.

## Macaroons

4   egg whites
½   teaspoon salt
2   cups sugar
½   cup blanched almonds, finely ground
1   teaspoon almond extract

Beat egg whites and salt until they are creamy. Add sugar a little at a time; then beat until peaks are formed. Fold in ground almonds and almond extract. Drop by spoonfuls onto cookie sheets (¾ inch apart) lined with unglazed paper. Bake in a preheated 350° oven for about 10 to 12 minutes, until light brown. Makes about 5 dozen macaroons.

66 Money isn't the most important thing in life. *People* are important. No Brink's truck is going to follow me to my grave. 99

# Festive Fondue

ITALIAN CHEESE FONDUE
FRENCH BREAD CUBES
ITALIAN ANCHOVY SALAD
SPUMONI ICE CREAM

*

SERVES 4

## Italian Cheese Fondue

3½  cups milk
  1  to 1½ pounds Fontina
     cheese
  5  tablespoons flour
     Salt and pepper to taste
  2  cloves garlic, minced
  ¼  cup kirsch

Heat milk in top of a double boiler. Grate cheese on coarse side of grater. Bring milk to boiling point. Shake grated cheese in a paper bag with flour, salt, pepper and garlic. Add a handful at a time to the boiling milk and stir. Keep adding cheese mixture until all is used. Add kirsch and stir well. Place in fondue pot. Keep hot; guests help themselves by dipping French Bread Cubes into fondue.

## French Bread Cubes

  3  eggs
  1  tablespoon grated Parmesan
     cheese
  1  teaspoon salt
  ½  teaspoon pepper
  ⅛  teaspoon oregano
  1  clove garlic, minced
  8  slices French bread
  1  cup oil

Beat eggs. Add cheese, salt, pepper, oregano and garlic; mix well. Cut bread into 1-inch cubes. Dip into egg mixture. Heat oil in an 8-inch skillet. Drop in cubes and fry on all sides until golden brown. Serve with fondue.

## Italian Anchovy Salad

  1  head lettuce, chopped
  1  teaspoon salt
  ¼  teaspoon pepper
  ⅛  teaspoon oregano
  1  clove garlic, minced
  1  (2-ounce) can anchovies,
     drained and cut into pieces
  1  small onion, finely chopped
  5  tablespoons oil
  1  tablespoon vinegar
  1  tablespoon grated Parmesan
     cheese (optional)

Place lettuce in a salad bowl. Sprinkle on salt, pepper, oregano and garlic. Add anchovies and onion. Shake oil and vinegar together in a small jar and drizzle over salad; toss lightly. Sprinkle with cheese for added flavor.

## Spumoni Ice Cream

1 cup milk
½ cup sugar
¼ teaspoon salt
4 egg yolks, beaten
1 square unsweetened
   chocolate
2 cups whipping cream
2 teaspoons rum extract
2 tablespoons sugar
⅛ teaspoon pistachio extract or
   ¼ cup pistachio nuts
2 or 3 drops green food coloring
1 (4-ounce) jar maraschino
   cherries, drained, chopped
   and chilled
6 almonds, finely chopped
½ teaspoon almond extract

Chill a bowl, rotary beater and 1-quart mold. Scald milk in top of double boiler. Stir in ½ cup sugar and the salt. Stir 3 tablespoons of the hot mixture into the beaten egg yolks. Immediately pour back into mixture in top of double boiler. Cook over simmering water until mixture coats spoon; remove from heat and cool.

Melt chocolate and set aside. Stir 1 cup whipping cream into custard mixture. Divide mixture between 2 bowls. Add melted chocolate to one bowl; mix well and place in refrigerator.

Add rum extract to mixture in second bowl; pour into refrigerator tray and freeze until mushy. Remove and put in a bowl. Beat with a chilled rotary beater until smooth and creamy. Put into chilled mold and freeze until firm.

Beat ½ cup whipping cream until it stands in peaks. Add 1 tablespoon sugar and the pistachio extract. Fold in green food coloring. Spoon pistachio mixture over frozen rum ice cream. Return to freezer. When firm, spread chopped maraschino cherries on top. Return to freezer.

Beat remaining ½ cup whipping cream in a chilled bowl with rotary beater until it stands up in peaks. Fold in remaining tablespoon sugar, the chopped almonds and almond extract. Spoon almond mixture over pistachio ice cream and maraschino cherries. Return to freezer. When almond ice cream is firm, pour chocolate mixture into refrigerator tray. Freeze until mushy. Put into chilled bowl and beat until creamy and smooth. Spoon mixture over almond ice cream.

Cover mold with plastic wrap and return to freezing compartment for 8 hours, or until firm. To unmold ice cream, dip mold into warm water for a few seconds.

66When you pick up a cheese and see drops of moisture on it (my grandfather used to call them "tears"), you know you have a good cheese. 99

57

# Popular Veal Parmesan

**VEAL PARMESAN**
**ACORN SQUASH**
**BEAN AND POTATO SALAD**
**MAMA D'S HOMEMADE BREAD**
**BISCUIT TORTONI**

\*

**SERVES 4**

## Veal Parmesan

1½  pounds veal (cut from the leg or shoulder), sliced ¼ inch thick
1  cup bread crumbs
   Grated Parmesan cheese
1  clove garlic, minced
½  teaspoon salt
⅛  teaspoon pepper
⅛  teaspoon oregano
½  cup oil
2  eggs, beaten
   Tomato sauce
   Grated mozzarella cheese

Cut the veal into 3x3-inch pieces. Mix bread crumbs, ¼ cup Parmesan cheese, the garlic, salt, pepper and oregano. Heat oil in a skillet. Dip veal in beaten eggs, then in bread crumb mixture; fry until golden brown on both sides.

Arrange veal on a lightly greased cookie sheet or baking dish. Spoon a little tomato sauce over each piece; sprinkle with additional Parmesan cheese and the grated mozzarella. Before serving, bake in a 375° oven for 15 minutes or until cheese is melted.

## Acorn Squash

2  acorn squash
4  tablespoons brown sugar
4  tablespoons butter

Cut squash in half and remove seeds. Put 1 tablespoon brown sugar and 1 tablespoon butter in each half. Place, cut sides up, in a baking pan. Pour water to ¾-inch depth around the squash and bake at 375° for 1 hour, or until tender.

## Bean and Potato Salad

1  (20-ounce) can green beans or 1 pound fresh green beans, cooked
2  small potatoes, cooked and mashed
2  tablespoons oil
   Salt and pepper to taste
1  clove garlic, minced
   Pinch of oregano
2  tablespoons grated Parmesan cheese

Heat beans, then drain. Add potatoes, oil, salt, pepper, garlic, oregano and cheese. Toss together lightly. Serve hot or cold.

58

## Mama D's Homemade Bread

1 package dry yeast
1 cup warm water
7½ cups flour
1 teaspoon salt
1 teaspoon sugar
⅓ cup oil
  Warm water

Dissolve yeast in warm water (water too hot or cold will kill the action of the yeast). Mix flour, salt and sugar. Make a well in the center of the flour mixture and add oil. Add yeast mixture and mix thoroughly. Gradually add more warm water to the dough, blending thoroughly until dough has an elastic consistency. Knead until an indentation in the dough will spring back. Cover and let rise until the dough doubles in size. Shape into 2 loaves and place on a greased baking sheet or in greased 9x5x3-inch bread pans; let rise until doubled again. Bake in a preheated 375° oven for 45 minutes to 1 hour.

## Biscuit Tortoni

½ cup crushed toasted almonds
½ cup crushed macaroons
2 cups heavy cream
3 tablespoons dark rum
¼ cup confectioners' sugar
3 or 4 maraschino cherries, halved

Reserve 2 tablespoons crushed toasted almonds for topping. Mix remaining crushed almonds, macaroons and 1 cup of the cream. Whip the remaining cup of cream with the rum and sugar. Fold into almond-macaroon mixture. Spoon into 6 or 8 paper dessert cups and freeze until hard. Top each with a cherry half, sprinkle with toasted almonds and return to freezer until ready to serve.

66 People should worry more about all the chemicals that go into their stomachs from the prepared foods they buy in the store. Just think about bread. Sometimes 17 percent of it is enriched, but 35 percent of the good stuff was taken out when the chemicals were put in. And the bugs won't even go near the chemicals. So you figure it out. 99

59

# Homestyle Barbecued Ribs

**BARBECUED SPARERIBS WITH JENNY'S FAVORITE BARBECUE SAUCE**

**ZUCCHINI CASSEROLE**

**RADISH SALAD**

**BREAD AND BUTTER**

**ALMOND BREAD PUDDING**

*

**SERVES 4**

## Barbecued Spareribs

 3  pounds lean spareribs
 ¼  cup oil
 3  onions, sliced and separated
     into rings
     Salt to taste
 ¼  teaspoon pepper
 ½  teaspoon oregano
 2  cloves garlic, minced
 1  teaspoon rosemary
     Jenny's Favorite Barbecue
     Sauce (below)

Rub ribs with oil and place in baking pan. Scatter onion rings over top and season with salt, pepper, oregano, garlic and rosemary. Brown slightly on both sides in a 375° oven. Drain off fat and pour Barbecue Sauce over the ribs. Lower heat to 350° and bake for about 1¾ hours, basting often.

## Jenny's Favorite Barbecue Sauce

 ¼  cup oil
 2  cloves garlic, minced
 2  onions, chopped
 1  (29-ounce) can tomato puree
 2  tablespoons wine vinegar
 2  tablespoons brown sugar
     Pinch of salt
 ½  teaspoon pepper
 ¼  teaspoon oregano

Heat oil in saucepan. Add garlic and onions and sauté lightly. Add remaining ingredients and stir. Simmer for 30 minutes.

## Zucchini Casserole

 4  or 5 small zucchini
 ¼  cup oil
 2  onions, chopped
 2  cloves garlic, minced
     Pinch of salt
 ½  teaspoon pepper
 ¼  teaspoon oregano
 1  (4-ounce) can sliced
     mushrooms, drained
 ¼  cup grated Parmesan cheese
 ¼  cup coarsely grated
     mozzarella cheese

Cut zucchini crosswise into 1-inch slices. Cook in salted boiling water until tender. Don't overcook. Drain. Heat oil in a saucepan and sauté onions and garlic. Add salt, pepper, oregano and mushrooms and sauté for 5 minutes. Add zucchini and Parmesan cheese. Transfer to an ungreased casserole, sprinkle with mozzarella cheese and bake, covered, in a 375° oven until cheese melts. Serve hot.

## Radish Salad

2   small bags radishes, sliced
¼   cup oil
1   tablespoon wine vinegar
    Pinch of salt
¼   teaspoon pepper
1   (2-ounce) bottle capers,
    drained
1   green pepper, cut into thin
    strips
2   stalks celery, thinly sliced

Mix all ingredients together in a salad bowl and toss gently. Taste for seasoning.

## Almond Bread Pudding

3½   cups milk
 ½   cup butter
 2   cups dry stale bread, cut into
     cubes
 ¾   cup sugar
 3   eggs, beaten
 1   teaspoon vanilla
 1   teaspoon cinnamon
 1   teaspoon mace
 1   teaspoon nutmeg
 1   cup raisins
 1   cup blanched almonds,
     chopped

Scald milk and add butter. Stir until butter is melted. Put bread in a mixing bowl and pour milk-butter mixture over bread. Soak for 7 minutes. Add remaining ingredients. (If raisins are dry, soak in warm water and drain before adding.) Mix together well. Pour into buttered casserole or baking dish. Set in a pan of hot water. Bake in a preheated 375° oven for 1 hour or until knife inserted in center of pudding comes out clean. Serve warm or cold.

66Peel large zucchini squash. Usually they're a little tough. The big ones are delicious sliced, dipped in egg and then in flour seasoned with salt, pepper, oregano, garlic and a little grated Parmesan cheese, and then fried. They're really delicious.99

# Dollar- Stretching Dinner

**MEAT LOAF ITALIAN STYLE**
**MASHED POTATOES ROMANO**
**PEAS WITH PROSCIUTTO**
**TOMATOES WITH BASIL**
**BREAD AND BUTTER**
**ALMOND COOKIES**
*
**SERVES 4 TO 6**

## Meat Loaf Italian Style

¼  cup oil
1  pound ground beef
1  pound ground pork
1  clove garlic, minced
8  sprigs parsley, finely chopped
4  eggs
4  slices dry bread, soaked in water and squeezed
¾  cup grated Romano cheese
Salt to taste
½  teaspoon pepper
4  hard-cooked eggs

Mix all ingredients except hard-cooked eggs in a bowl. Grease a loaf pan. Shape half the meat into an oblong or oval shape in the pan. Arrange hard-cooked eggs lengthwise down the center. Oil your hands and cover eggs completely with remaining meat. Smooth meat with oiled hands; bake in a 375° oven for 1 hour.

## Mashed Potatoes Romano

6  potatoes, boiled and mashed
3  tablespoons grated Romano cheese
Butter
¼  cup milk
Salt to taste
Paprika

Mix together mashed potatoes, cheese, 2 tablespoons butter, the milk and salt. Put in a round baking dish. Dot with additional butter and sprinkle with paprika. Bake in a 375° oven until golden brown, about 35 minutes.

## Peas with Prosciutto

2  tablespoons butter
¼  pound prosciutto ham, sliced thin and chopped
4  scallions, diced
Salt to taste
½  teaspoon pepper
6  sprigs parsley, finely chopped
1  (16-ounce) can peas or
1 pound fresh peas

Put butter, prosciutto, scallions, salt, pepper and parsley in skillet and simmer for 5 minutes. Add peas and cook slowly for 10 minutes. Adjust cooking time for fresh peas.

## Tomatoes with Basil

4 tomatoes, sliced
1 clove garlic, minced
   Salt to taste
½ teaspoon pepper
¼ teaspoon oregano
1 teaspoon basil
2 tablespoons grated Romano
   cheese
2 tablespoons oil

Arrange tomatoes on a platter. Sprinkle with minced garlic, salt, pepper, oregano, basil and cheese. Drizzle oil over all.

## Almond Cookies

3 eggs
1 cup sugar
   Juice and grated rind
   of 1 lemon
1 teaspoon vanilla
½ cup milk
2 cups flour
3 teaspoons baking powder
½ cup shortening
½ cup almonds, chopped

Cream eggs and sugar together. Add lemon juice, vanilla and ¼ cup of the milk. Mix flour and baking powder together and cut in shortening. Add almonds and grated lemon rind to flour-shortening mixture; add this to egg mixture alternately with remaining ¼ cup milk, mixing well. Make 3 or 4 long rolls, 2 inches thick. Place on a greased cookie sheet and bake in a preheated 325° oven for 25 to 30 minutes. Remove from cookie sheet and slice at an angle into ½-inch slices. Makes 5 to 6 dozen cookies.

66 I've seen people throw the green part of green onions away. I can't say enough times, "Waste not—want not." Chop the tops up sometime. Put them in olive oil and brown them a little. Then add eggs to them, cook, and see how they taste. Delicious. 99

63

# Good Soup for Supper

MINESTRONE

TUNA FISH AND
VEGETABLE SALAD

GARLIC BREAD (PAGE 71)

ITALIAN RUM CAKE (PAGE 43)

*

SERVES 4

## Minestrone

1   pound dried white beans
    (Great Northern or other
    white beans)
4   stalks celery, sliced
4   carrots, diced
2   potatoes, peeled and diced
4   sprigs parsley, chopped
1   (16-ounce) can chick-peas
    (garbanzos)
    Salt and pepper to taste
½   cup oil
2   onions, diced
4   cloves garlic, minced
8   sprigs parsley, chopped
    Salt and pepper to taste
3   or 4 ripe tomatoes, chopped
1   medium zucchini, diced

Fill a large pot (6 to 8 quarts) with water to 4 inches from top. Wash the beans thoroughly and cook until tender. When beans are tender, replace the water lost in cooking and return to a boil. Add celery, carrots, potatoes, 4 sprigs parsley, chopped, the chick-peas, salt and pepper.

Heat oil in a small saucepan. Add onions, garlic, 8 sprigs parsley, chopped, salt and pepper and sauté until the onions are golden brown. Add tomatoes and cook for 20 to 30 minutes over medium-low heat. Add to beans and vegetables; cook slowly for an additional 2½ to 3 hours. Add diced zucchini just before final 20 minutes of cooking.

Note: This recipe makes enough for 20 or more servings. Freeze leftover soup for future meals.

## Tuna Fish and Vegetable Salad

½   head lettuce, cut into chunks
1   (6-ounce) can tuna fish (either
    flaked or solid pack), drained
1   small cucumber, thinly sliced
2   or 3 stalks celery, sliced (use
    leaves, too)
1   clove garlic, minced
1   small onion, chopped
    Salt and pepper to taste
3   tablespoons oil
1   tablespoon wine vinegar
    Lemon juice to taste
1   tablespoon grated Parmesan
    cheese

Place lettuce, tuna fish, cucumber, celery, garlic, onion, salt and pepper in a bowl and toss. Put oil and vinegar in a small jar and shake well. Drizzle dressing and lemon juice over salad. Sprinkle cheese on top. Taste for seasoning.

Minestrone (page 64)

Ricotta and Strawberry Crepes (page 67)

Right after adding batter, tilt pan to spread batter evenly.

Combine ricotta mixture and strawberries; spoon onto crepes.

Roll up filled crepes; sprinkle with confectioners' sugar. Then enjoy!

## Oven-Baked Beef Stew

3 pounds beef, cubed
1 teaspoon basil
6 carrots, quartered
6 small potatoes, peeled
4 stalks celery, halved
3 onions, chopped
  Salt to taste
½ teaspoon pepper
¼ teaspoon oregano
4 or 5 ripe tomatoes (fresh or canned), crushed
¼ cup oil

Put all the ingredients except the oil in a roasting pan. Sprinkle with the oil; toss gently. Bake in a 350° oven for 2¼ hours, basting often, until meat is tender. Taste to see if you should add more seasonings.

## Olive and Eggplant Salad

1 large eggplant, peeled and sliced
1 small onion, chopped
  Pinch of salt
½ teaspoon pepper
¼ teaspoon oregano
1 clove garlic, minced
¼ pound black Italian olives
2 tomatoes, cut into wedges
3 sprigs parsley, chopped
¼ cup oil
1 tablespoon plus 1 teaspoon wine vinegar

Cut eggplant slices into pieces; cook in boiling salted water until tender. Drain and squeeze dry. Combine with remaining ingredients and toss gently.

## Old-Fashioned Apple Pie

2 cups flour
1 teaspoon salt
⅔ cup lard
6 tablespoons cold water
6 or 7 large cooking apples
1 cup sugar
1 teaspoon cinnamon
3 tablespoons butter, cut up
  Milk
  Sugar

Mix flour and salt together. Add lard and crumble with fingers into flour. Add water. Work with your hands quickly to form a ball. Add more water if necessary. Roll out pastry for 2 crusts.

Peel and core apples and slice thinly. Put in a bowl. Add 1 cup sugar and the cinnamon; mix thoroughly. Line a 9-inch pie pan with pastry; add apple mixture. Sprinkle butter over the apples. Put the second pastry circle on the pie; trim excess pastry. Make indentations all around edge of pastry with a fork. Prick top pastry with fork to make air holes. Bake in a preheated 375° oven for 10 minutes. Lower heat to 350° and bake for 30 minutes more. Brush pie with a little milk and sprinkle with sugar. Return to oven and bake for 10 more minutes.

# Informal Winter Buffet

OVEN-BAKED BEEF STEW
OLIVE AND EGGPLANT SALAD
BREAD AND BUTTER
OLD-FASHIONED APPLE PIE
*
SERVES 6 TO 8

# Celebration Dinner

**GNOCCHI WITH GARLIC BUTTER OR BOLOGNESE TOMATO SAUCE**

**ROAST STUFFED CHICKEN**

**ITALIAN SALAD (PAGE 81)**

**BREAD AND BUTTER**

**RICOTTA AND STRAWBERRY CREPES**

*

**SERVES 6**

## Gnocchi

6   large potatoes (unpeeled)
2   eggs, beaten
2   tablespoons oil or butter
1   teaspoon salt
½   cup grated Parmesan cheese
1   to 1½ cups flour
    Garlic Butter (below) or
    Bolognese Tomato Sauce
    (right)

Boil potatoes in their jackets until tender; peel. Mash or put through a potato ricer. Blend in eggs, oil, salt and cheese. Then add flour, a little at a time, until all is blended together. Knead dough lightly on a floured board and form into little ropes, 1 inch in diameter. Cut each rope into pieces ¾ inch long. Cook in salted boiling water until gnocchi rise to top of water. Cook a little longer, 2 to 3 minutes. Drain and serve with Garlic Butter or Bolognese Tomato Sauce.

## *Garlic Butter*

    Salt, pepper and oregano to
    taste
¼   teaspoon garlic powder or
    1 clove garlic, mashed
1   cup (½ pound) butter, melted
    Grated Parmesan cheese

Add salt, pepper, oregano and garlic powder to butter. Pour over gnocchi and toss lightly. Spoon onto a serving platter and sprinkle with cheese. Serve hot.

## *Bolognese Tomato Sauce*

¼   cup oil
1   onion, diced
¼   pound salt pork, diced
½   pound hot or mild sausages, sliced
½   pound beef, cubed
    Salt to taste
2   cloves garlic, minced
1   teaspoon basil
¼   teaspoon pepper
1   teaspoon dried parsley
1   bay leaf
1   (29-ounce) can tomatoes, crushed
1   (6-ounce) can tomato paste
1   (6-ounce) can water
½   cup dry white wine
1   (4-ounce) can mushrooms (undrained)

Heat oil in a saucepan. Add onion and salt pork and sauté until onion is golden brown. Add sausages and beef and brown slowly. Add salt, garlic, basil, pepper, parsley, bay leaf, tomatoes, tomato paste and water. Stir well. Add wine and mushrooms. Cook slowly for 2 hours. Serve over gnocchi or any pasta of your choice.

## Roast Stuffed Chicken

1 plump chicken (3 to 3½ pounds)
  Salt, pepper and oregano to taste
2 cloves garlic, minced
¼ cup oil
2 small onions, chopped
2 stalks celery, chopped
2 cloves garlic, minced
¾ pound ground pork
1 teaspoon fennel seed
1 teaspoon salt
4 slices bread, soaked in water and squeezed
2 eggs, beaten
½ cup grated Parmesan cheese
  Oil or butter

Rub chicken with salt inside and out. Rinse under cold water. Season cavity with salt, pepper, oregano and 2 cloves garlic, minced.

Heat ¼ cup oil in a large skillet and brown onions, celery and 2 cloves garlic, minced. Season with salt, pepper and oregano. Remove with slotted spoon and set aside in a bowl, leaving the oil in the skillet. Mix together the pork, fennel seed and 1 teaspoon salt. Add the pork mixture to the skillet; cook until brown. Add to the bowl with the onion mixture. Stir in the bread, eggs and cheese. Mix together well and taste for seasoning.

Fill the chicken cavity with stuffing. Sew or use skewers to hold stuffing in place; truss the chicken. Rub all over with oil. Place in a roasting pan; roast in a 375° oven for about 1 hour or until tender. Cover the roaster for the last 15 or 20 minutes of cooking. Baste the chicken often with its own juices.

## Ricotta and Strawberry Crepes

2 tablespoons butter
½ cup sifted flour
2 eggs plus 2 egg yolks, beaten
2 cups milk
1 tablespoon granulated sugar
  Pinch of salt
⅔ pound ricotta cheese
¼ cup granulated sugar
1 teaspoon vanilla
1 pint strawberries, hulled and crushed
  Confectioners' sugar

Melt butter in top of a double boiler. Mix flour, eggs and yolks, milk, 1 tablespoon granulated sugar and the salt; blend well. Heat a 6-inch skillet or 6-inch crepe pan; brush with melted butter. Pour in about 3 tablespoons batter and spread over entire pan. Cook crepe on both sides. Stack crepes as they are cooked; cover them with waxed paper until you're ready to fill them.

Cream the ricotta with ¼ cup granulated sugar and the vanilla. Add strawberries and mix gently. Spoon mixture down center of each crepe and roll it up. Sprinkle with confectioners' sugar.

66 There is the difference of night and day between fresh and prepared herbs. You never know how long prepared herbs have been in the containers. So use the fresh herbs whenever you can. 99

# Dinner for an Autumn Day

**PORK SHANKS WITH
TOMATO SAUCE**

**FETTUCCINE**

**CELERY-BEET SALAD**

**BREAD AND BUTTER**

**APPLE FRITTERS**

*

**SERVES 4**

## Pork Shanks with Tomato Sauce

8 small pork shanks
  Salt
¼ teaspoon pepper
⅛ teaspoon oregano
  Garlic powder to taste
¼ cup oil
1 onion, finely chopped
2 cloves garlic, minced
¼ cup oil
¼ teaspoon pepper
⅛ teaspoon oregano
1 bay leaf
2 (29-ounce) cans Italian
  tomatoes, crushed
1 (6-ounce) can tomato paste
2 (6-ounce) cans water

Season pork shanks with salt, ¼ teaspoon pepper, ⅛ teaspoon oregano and the garlic powder. Add ¼ cup oil, toss together and put in a baking pan. Roast in a 375° oven for about 45 minutes, until golden brown. Remove and set aside.

Brown onion and garlic in ¼ cup oil in a Dutch oven. Add salt, ¼ teaspoon pepper, ⅛ teaspoon oregano and the bay leaf. Sauté for a few minutes. Add tomatoes, tomato paste and water. Simmer slowly for 15 minutes, then add pork shanks and cook slowly for 2½ hours. Remove and discard bay leaf. Serve pork shanks separately; serve tomato sauce over fettuccine.

## Fettuccine

6 quarts water
1 tablespoon salt
1 pound fettuccine
1 tablespoon oil
¼ cup grated Romano cheese

Bring water and salt to a rolling boil in large pot; add fettuccine and oil. Cook until *al dente*. (Taste and test—don't overcook.) Drain in colander and place on large serving platter. Sprinkle with cheese and pour sauce from pork shanks over pasta.

## Celery-Beet Salad

4 stalks celery, diced
2 hard-cooked eggs, sliced
1 clove garlic, minced
   Pinch of salt
½ teaspoon pepper
1 (29-ounce) can sliced beets, drained
6 tablespoons oil
1 tablespoon wine vinegar

Mix all ingredients except oil and vinegar together. Add oil and vinegar. Toss gently and serve.

## Apple Fritters

¼ teaspoon salt
1½ cups flour
3 tablespoons sugar
3 eggs, beaten
½ teaspoon cinnamon
1 cup milk or water
1 tablespoon melted butter or oil
3 apples, chopped or thinly sliced (unpeeled)
   Oil for frying
   Cinnamon
   Sugar

Mix salt, flour, 3 tablespoons sugar, the eggs, ½ teaspoon cinnamon, the milk and melted butter in a bowl. It should have the consistency of pancake batter. Add a little more milk or flour if necessary. Add apples and mix well. Heat about 1 inch of oil in a skillet. Drop batter by tablespoonfuls into the hot oil; brown on both sides. Drain on paper towels and sprinkle with a mixture of cinnamon and sugar.

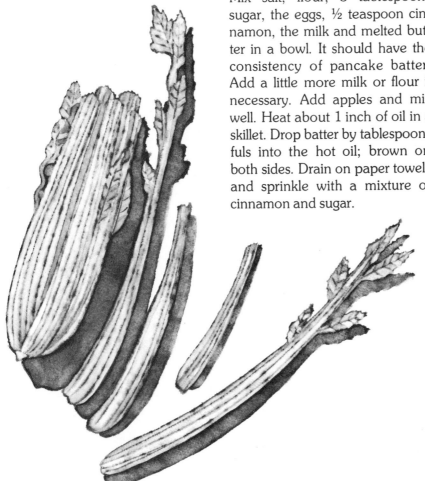

66 When a well-known cookbook authority wrote a new cookbook, one of the critics asked why it was so lengthy. And she replied that it was for the new cooks. I say that new cooks are scared away from cooking when they see such lengthy recipes, with all those ingredients they've never heard of. Some simple ingredient will do the same thing most of the time. 99

# Pasta With a Difference

RIGATONI WITH
SAUSAGE SAUCE

CURLY ENDIVE SALAD

GARLIC BREAD

ALMOND SLICES

*

SERVES 6

## Rigatoni with Sausage Sauce

6 quarts water
1 tablespoon salt
1 pound rigatoni
   Grated Romano cheese
   Sausage Sauce (below)

Bring water and salt to a rolling boil in a large pot; add rigatoni and cook for about 20 minutes, until *al dente*—don't overcook. Drain, sprinkle with cheese and mix with Sausage Sauce.

### Sausage Sauce

1 pound Italian sausages
1 onion, chopped
2 cloves garlic, minced
1 (29-ounce) can Italian tomatoes, crushed
1 (6-ounce) can tomato paste
1 (6-ounce) can water
1 teaspoon basil
  Pinch of salt
¼ teaspoon pepper
⅛ teaspoon oregano
2 (4-ounce) cans mushrooms

Put sausages in a baking pan and bake at 375° for 20 minutes. Remove sausages and cut into serving pieces. Using fat from sausages, sauté onion and garlic until lightly browned. Add tomatoes, tomato paste, water, basil, salt, pepper and oregano. Add mushrooms and simmer, uncovered, for 2 hours, stirring occasionally.

## Curly Endive Salad

1 head curly endive
3 or 4 potatoes, boiled, peeled
   and sliced
2 hard-cooked eggs, cut in
   half lengthwise
   Pinch of salt
¼ teaspoon pepper
⅛ teaspoon oregano
1 clove garlic, minced
   Juice of 1 lemon
¼ cup oil

Wash endive and pat dry with paper towels. Remove tough outer leaves. Cut endive coarsely and place in a salad bowl. Add potato slices and eggs. Season with salt, pepper, oregano and garlic. Squeeze lemon juice over salad and sprinkle with oil. Toss gently and serve.

## Garlic Bread

Cut a loaf of French bread into ½-inch slices, but do not cut all the way through. Butter slices generously. Sprinkle with garlic powder and grated Romano cheese. Put into a brown paper bag and bake in a preheated 325° oven for about 15 to 20 minutes. Serve warm.

## Almond Slices

4 eggs, beaten
1¼ cups sugar
½ cup oil
½ cup chopped almonds
   Juice and grated rind
   of 1 lemon
1½ teaspoons vanilla
½ teaspoon almond extract
3 teaspoons baking powder
3 cups flour

Mix eggs and sugar. Add oil, almonds, lemon juice and grated rind, vanilla and almond extract. Mix baking powder and flour together. Add to egg and sugar mixture. Knead and roll out into long rolls 2 inches thick. Place rolls on greased and floured cookie sheets. Bake in a preheated 325° oven for about 25 minutes. Remove from pans and cut into ½-inch slices. Makes 6 to 8 dozen cookies.

66 Waste not—you want not. Save your bread. It's a sin to throw it away when you can make bread puddings and so many different things out of it. Also, you save money every time you make your own seasoned bread crumbs. 99

# For a Special Occasion

## VEAL ROAST WITH CARROTS AND POTATOES

## MUSHROOMS WITH GARLIC AND ONION

## ZUCCHINI AND ANCHOVY SALAD

## BREAD AND BUTTER

## STEWED APPLES WITH CINNAMON

*

### SERVES 4 TO 6

## Veal Roast with Carrots and Potatoes

3- pound veal shoulder or rump roast
¼ pound bacon, cut into small pieces
  Pinch of salt
½ teaspoon pepper
¼ teaspoon oregano
2 cloves garlic, minced
3 sprigs parsley, finely chopped, or 1 teaspoon dried parsley
¼ cup oil
3 medium onions, quartered
6 carrots, quartered
4 to 6 medium potatoes, quartered
1 cup water

Cut slits in veal with sharp knife. Put a piece of bacon in each slit. Mix salt, pepper, oregano, garlic and parsley together. Put a little of the mixture into each slit. Heat oil in a roasting pan and brown veal on all sides. Remove from top of stove. Arrange vegetables around the browned veal, add water, cover and roast in a 350° oven for 2½ to 3 hours.

## Mushrooms with Garlic and Onion

½ cup oil
1 green pepper, diced
1 large clove garlic, minced
2 onions, chopped
1 pound fresh mushrooms, sliced, or 2 (8-ounce) cans sliced mushrooms, drained
  Salt to taste
½ teaspoon pepper
¼ teaspoon oregano

Heat oil in saucepan; add green pepper, garlic and onions. Sauté gently. Add mushrooms, salt, pepper and oregano. Simmer, uncovered, on low heat, stirring occasionally, for 15 minutes. May be served hot or cold.

72

## Zucchini and Anchovy Salad

6 small zucchini
2 small onions, thinly sliced
1 (2-ounce) can anchovies, drained
  Pinch of salt
¼ teaspoon pepper
1 clove garlic, minced
2 tablespoons wine vinegar
½ cup oil
1 tablespoon grated Romano cheese

Cook zucchini in boiling water about 7 minutes, until barely tender. Drain and cut into ½-inch slices. Put into bowl and add onions and anchovies. Add salt, pepper and garlic. Mix vinegar and oil and sprinkle over salad. Sprinkle cheese on top.

## Stewed Apples with Cinnamon

4 to 6 cooking apples
1½ cups water
5 tablespoons sugar
2 tablespoons butter
1 teaspoon cinnamon

Peel apples and cut into wedges ½ inch thick. Put water in saucepan. Add apples, cover and cook over low heat until tender. Add sugar and simmer uncovered a few minutes. Mix in butter and cinnamon. Cool and serve.

"Learn to measure with your hands and your eyes when you're cooking. You don't have to measure everything out, a tablespoon of this and a teaspoon of that. Taste, taste, taste. I have to laugh when recipes say, "Add 1 teaspoon salt." How do they know the quality of the salt? Some salt is so bad, you can add a ton of it and still never season your food properly. Other kinds, you can add just a little bit."

# Cold-Weather Treat

**DUCK WITH MOSTACCIOLI**

**GREEN BEANS WITH ALMONDS (PAGE 6)**

**ARTICHOKE SALAD**

**RICOTTA CHEESE PUDDING**

\*

**SERVES 4**

## Duck with Mostaccioli

3- to 4-pound duckling
2 tablespoons butter
1 onion, diced
2 cloves garlic, minced
2 (29-ounce) cans Italian
    tomatoes, crushed
    Pinch of salt
½ teaspoon pepper
⅛ teaspoon oregano
½ cup red wine
1 bay leaf
    Mostaccioli (right)
¼ cup grated Parmesan or
    Romano cheese

Clean duck and cut into serving pieces. Brown duck on all sides in butter, then transfer to a large baking pan. Brown onion and garlic in same butter. Add tomatoes and simmer for 5 minutes, then pour over duck. Add salt, pepper, oregano, wine and bay leaf. Bake, uncovered, in a 375° oven until duck is tender, about 1½ to 2 hours. Remove duck and bay leaf from sauce; discard bay leaf. Pour duck sauce over mostaccioli and sprinkle with cheese. Serve duck with the mostaccioli on a heated platter.

## Mostaccioli

6 quarts water
1 tablespoon salt
1 pound mostaccioli

Bring water and salt to rolling boil in large pot; add mostaccioli. Stir and cook until mostaccioli is slightly chewy (*al dente*). Drain in colander.

## Artichoke Salad

1 (14-ounce) can baby
   artichoke hearts, drained
   Pinch of salt
½ teaspoon pepper
¼ teaspoon oregano
1 clove garlic, minced
¼ cup oil
   Lemon wedges

Put artichoke hearts in a bowl and season with salt, pepper, oregano and garlic. Pour oil over all and toss gently. Serve with lemon wedges.

## Ricotta Cheese Pudding

¼ cup white raisins
6 tablespoons candied mixed
   peels
¼ cup rum
2 tablespoons butter
   Dry bread crumbs
5 eggs
1½ pounds ricotta cheese, put
   through fine sieve
5 teaspoons flour
6 tablespoons confectioners'
   sugar
½ teaspoon cinnamon

Soak raisins and peels in rum. Butter a baking dish and shake in enough bread crumbs to coat the buttered dish. Separate 4 of the eggs. Beat 4 egg yolks and 1 whole egg until smooth. Beat 4 egg whites separately until stiff. Put sieved ricotta in a bowl; add yolks, flour, raisins, candied peels, rum, sugar and cinnamon. Taste. If not sweet enough, add more sugar. Fold in egg whites. Fill baking dish half full. Bake in a preheated 375° oven for 1 hour. Serve hot or cold.

Note: This recipe makes enough to serve 4 to 6 people generously, so you might have some left over. Just refrigerate it—it's delicious the next day, too!

66 The trouble with American cooking is that we want to cook everything *fast* and get done with it. European women don't cook that way. My sister-in-law, who was an excellent cook, would take all day to prepare a meal. She didn't spend all that time standing over the stove, but she'd cook the food for a long time, as slowly as possible. Every once in a while she'd go into the kitchen and stir what was cooking.99

# Extra-Special Eggplant

**STUFFED EGGPLANT AND POTATOES**

**SPINACH AND EGG SALAD**

**LEMON CAKE**

\*

**SERVES 4**

## Stuffed Eggplant and Potatoes

2 medium eggplants
¼ cup oil
1 onion, chopped
2 cloves garlic, minced
Pinch of salt
¼ teaspoon pepper
⅛ teaspoon oregano
⅔ pound ground beef
2 eggs, beaten
2 slices day-old bread, soaked and squeezed dry
½ cup grated Romano cheese
2 large Idaho potatoes
Tomato Sauce (right)

Cut unpeeled eggplants in half and remove pulp, leaving shells ½ inch thick. Cook eggplant shells and pulp in boiling water for 15 minutes; drain.

Heat oil in a skillet. Brown onion and garlic. Add salt, pepper, oregano and ground beef. Cook for 5 to 7 minutes. Place meat mixture in a bowl. Add eggs, bread, cheese and chopped eggplant pulp; mix. Fill eggplant shells with meat mixture, reserving some of the mixture for potatoes, and place in a large greased baking pan.

Cut potatoes in half. Cut out most of potato pulp (leave intact). Fill potato shells with reserved meat mixture. Place stuffed potato shells, along with the scooped-out potato centers, in the baking pan. Pour Tomato Sauce over eggplants and potatoes. Bake in a 350° oven for 1 hour.

## Tomato Sauce

1 onion, chopped
1 clove garlic, minced
¼ cup oil
Salt to taste
¼ teaspoon pepper
⅛ teaspoon oregano
1 (29-ounce) can Italian tomatoes, crushed

Sauté onion and garlic in oil. Add salt, pepper, oregano and crushed tomatoes. Simmer for 20 minutes.

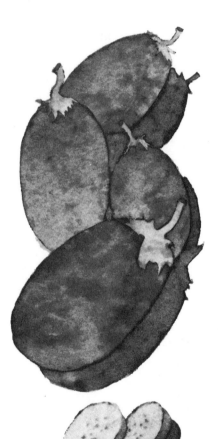

## Spinach and Egg Salad

1 to 1½ pounds spinach
1 clove garlic, minced
1 tablespoon lemon juice
  Pinch of salt
¼ teaspoon pepper
⅛ teaspoon oregano
2 hard-cooked eggs, sliced
2 small tomatoes, cut into
  wedges
1 small onion, sliced and
  separated into rings
¼ cup oil
1 tablespoon wine vinegar

Wash spinach; pat dry with paper towels. Remove tough stems and discard. Cut up spinach leaves. Place all ingredients except oil and vinegar in a salad bowl and toss gently. Mix oil and vinegar; pour over salad and toss.

## Lemon Cake

6 egg yolks, beaten
1 cup granulated sugar
  Grated rind of 1 lemon
¼ cup butter, melted
1¼ cups sifted cake flour
2 teaspoons baking powder
6 egg whites, beaten stiff
  Confectioners' sugar

Preheat oven to 350°. Grease and flour a tube cake pan. Put egg yolks, granulated sugar and lemon rind in top of double boiler (keep water hot in bottom, but not boiling). Beat mixture until it is lukewarm. Remove from heat. Add butter, flour and baking powder; mix well. Fold in stiffly beaten egg whites. Pour batter into a tube cake pan and bake for about 40 minutes. Remove cake and let cool. Sprinkle with confectioners' sugar when ready to serve.

66 Try different brands of coffee until you hit the blend you like. Select the grind for your kind of coffeepot. I still think the old enameled coffeepots make the best coffee. You really get the true coffee flavor when you put the coffee grounds right into the water. A good formula for coffee making that pleases most people is to add one tablespoon of coffee for each cup and then one extra tablespoon for the pot. 99

# The Flavor of Naples

**PORK CHOPS
NEAPOLITAN STYLE**

**BAKED POTATOES
ITALIAN STYLE**

**ASPARAGUS WITH ROMANO**

**CHICK-PEA SALAD**

**BREAD AND BUTTER**

**STRAWBERRIES IN WINE
(PAGE 24)**

\*

**SERVES 4**

## Pork Chops Neapolitan Style

2 cloves garlic, minced
¼ cup oil
4 pork chops, rib or loin
2 green peppers, chopped
1 teaspoon salt
¼ teaspoon pepper
   Scant pinch of oregano
2 fresh ripe tomatoes, chopped, or ½ cup crushed Italian tomatoes
3 tablespoons wine vinegar
1 (4-ounce) can mushrooms (undrained)

Brown garlic in oil in a skillet with a tight-fitting cover. Add pork chops and brown on both sides, adding chopped green peppers, salt, pepper, oregano, tomatoes, wine vinegar and mushrooms. Cover the skillet and cook the pork chops over low heat for about 45 minutes; add a little water as needed.

## Baked Potatoes Italian Style

5 medium baking potatoes, peeled
¼ cup oil
3 sprigs parsley, chopped
1 teaspoon salt
½ teaspoon pepper
⅛ teaspoon oregano
2 cloves garlic, minced

Cut each potato into 6 lengthwise slices. Mix potato slices, oil, parsley, salt, pepper, oregano and garlic in a bowl. Grease a baking pan. Add potatoes and bake at 375° until potatoes are tender and golden brown.

## Asparagus with Romano

1½ pounds fresh asparagus
½ cup (¼ pound) butter
2 cloves garlic, minced
1 teaspoon salt
½ teaspoon pepper
½ cup grated Romano cheese

Wash asparagus in cold water to remove sand. Snap off tough lower part of stalks. Cook in salted boiling water until barely tender. Drain and put into a greased casserole. Melt butter in a saucepan; add garlic, salt and pepper and simmer for a few minutes. Pour over asparagus and sprinkle with cheese. Bake at 375° for 10 minutes.

## Chick-Pea Salad

1 (16-ounce) can chick-peas (garbanzos), drained
4 stalks celery, chopped
1 onion, chopped
1 green pepper, chopped
1 fresh tomato, cut into wedges
Salt, pepper, oregano and minced garlic to taste
¼ cup oil
1 tablespoon wine vinegar

Mix together chick-peas, celery, onion, green pepper, tomato, salt, pepper, oregano and garlic. Put oil and vinegar into a jar and shake well. Pour over salad.

66 Pork chops with pockets are excellent stuffed with bread crumbs seasoned with salt, pepper, oregano and garlic. Add a little prosciutto ham, if you like.99

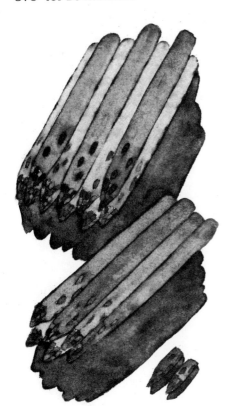

# Perfect Pasta

SPAGHETTI BOLOGNESE
ITALIAN SALAD
GARLIC BREAD (PAGE 71)
CANNOLI CAKE
PEACHES AND WINE

*

SERVES 4 TO 6

## Spaghetti Bolognese

½   cup oil
1   small onion, finely chopped
2   cloves garlic, minced
3   sprigs parsley, chopped
1   pound ground beef
     Salt and pepper to taste
¼   teaspoon oregano
½   teaspoon basil
1   (29-ounce) can plum
     tomatoes, crushed
1   (6-ounce) can tomato paste
1   cup water
6   quarts water
1   tablespoon salt
1   pound spaghetti
¼   cup grated Parmesan cheese

Put the oil, onion, garlic and parsley into a 2-quart saucepan. Sauté slowly. Add ground beef, salt and pepper to taste, oregano and basil. Sauté slowly, stirring often, until meat is brown. Add tomatoes, tomato paste and 1 cup water. Simmer slowly, uncovered, for approximately 2 hours, stirring occasionally.

Bring 6 quarts water and 1 tablespoon salt to rolling boil in a large pot. Add spaghetti, stirring frequently so it doesn't stick. Cook for about 10 minutes, until spaghetti is *al dente*, a little on the firm side. Drain well and put on a large platter. Sprinkle with cheese. Spoon hot sauce over spaghetti and serve.

Note: Other pastas can be substituted for spaghetti.

## Italian Salad

1 large head lettuce
½ onion, finely chopped
  Minced garlic
  Salt and pepper to taste
  Oregano (optional)
½ cup oil
2 tablespoons wine vinegar
1 tomato, cut into wedges

Break lettuce into a large salad bowl or individual bowls. Add onion and garlic. Shake on salt, pepper and oregano. Put oil and vinegar in a pint bottle or jar and shake well. Drizzle over salad; toss. Garnish with tomato wedges.

Note: If you have leftover salad dressing, refrigerate and use later.

## Cannoli Cake

1 (19-ounce) package lemon
  cake mix
½ cup oil
4 eggs
1 cup milk
2 cups ricotta cheese
¾ cup sugar
½ teaspoon cinnamon
1 teaspoon vanilla
  Maraschino cherries (optional)

Preheat oven to 375°. Combine cake mix, oil, eggs and milk and blend thoroughly; pour into a greased pan (either two 9-inch round layer pans or one 11x14-inch pan). Bake layers 25 to 30 minutes, rectangle 30 to 35 minutes. Cake is done when it pops back after being pressed lightly with a finger. Let cake cool.

Blend ricotta, sugar, cinnamon and vanilla; mix well. Spread over cooled cake. Dot with maraschino cherries for color, if desired.

## Peaches and Wine

1 (29-ounce) can sliced
  peaches
1½ to 2 cups dry wine

Divide peaches among 4 sherbet glasses. Sprinkle with a little of the peach syrup. Pour 1 inch of wine over the peaches. Chill and serve.

**"**It's impossible to tell anyone exactly how long to cook pasta. Spaghetti is not uniform and varies from brand to brand. That with the most durum wheat or semolina content takes the longest to cook. One pound of pasta will serve four to six.**"**

# Homemade Green Noodles

**SPINACH NOODLES WITH RAGU SAUCE**

**VEAL CUTLETS MILAN STYLE**

**FONTINA CHEESE AND PEPPER SALAD**

**HONEY COOKIES (PAGE 89)**

*

**SERVES 6**

## Spinach Noodles with Ragu Sauce

1 package frozen chopped spinach, cooked and thoroughly drained
4 cups flour
¾ teaspoon salt
3 eggs
3 tablespoons water
6 quarts water
1 tablespoon salt
Ragu Sauce (right)

Chop spinach very finely. Put flour in large bowl and make a well in the center. Add spinach, ¾ teaspoon salt, the eggs and 3 tablespoons water. Mix and knead until dough is stiff and elastic. Add a little more water if necessary. Do not over-knead. Divide into 3 parts and roll out paper thin on a floured board. Flour each sheet of dough; roll up like a jelly roll. Slice noodle dough with a sharp knife into ¼-inch strips. Shake strips out and put them on a floured board to dry for about 1 hour. (Makes about 2 pounds pasta.)

Bring 6 quarts water and 1 tablespoon salt to a rolling boil in a large pot. Add green noodles; cook until they are slightly chewy (*al dente*) —don't overcook. Drain in a colander. Serve with Ragu Sauce.

## Ragu Sauce

¼ cup oil
2 small onions, minced
2 cloves garlic, minced
1 (29-ounce) can Italian plum tomatoes, crushed
1 (6-ounce) can tomato paste
1 (6-ounce) can water
Salt to taste
½ teaspoon pepper
¼ teaspoon oregano
½ teaspoon basil

Heat oil in saucepan and sauté onions and garlic until golden. Add tomatoes, tomato paste, water, salt, pepper, oregano and basil. Cook sauce, uncovered, for 1½ hours over low heat, stirring occasionally.

## Veal Cutlets Milan Style

1½  pounds veal cutlets
 2  eggs
    Salt
 ¼  teaspoon pepper
 ⅛  teaspoon oregano
 1  clove garlic, minced
1½  cups bread crumbs
 ¼  cup grated Romano cheese
 ¼  teaspoon pepper
 ⅛  teaspoon oregano
 1  clove garlic, minced
 1  teaspoon dried parsley
    Butter or oil
    Lemon wedges

Pound cutlets on both sides. Beat eggs and add a pinch of salt, ¼ teaspoon pepper, ⅛ teaspoon oregano and 1 clove garlic, minced. Mix together bread crumbs, cheese, ¼ teaspoon pepper, salt to taste, ⅛ teaspoon oregano, 1 clove garlic, minced, and the dried parsley. Dip cutlets in egg mixture, then in seasoned bread crumbs, coating both sides. Fry in butter over medium heat until cutlets are golden brown on both sides. Serve hot, garnished with lemon wedges.

## Fontina Cheese and Pepper Salad

 3  green peppers, cut up
 ½  pound Fontina cheese, diced
 ½  cup whole green Italian olives
 ½  cup black olives
 1  clove garlic, minced
    Pinch of salt
 ½  teaspoon pepper
 ¼  teaspoon oregano
 ¼  cup oil
 1  tablespoon wine vinegar
 1  tablespoon grated Romano cheese

Mix together green peppers, Fontina cheese, green olives, black olives and garlic. Season with salt, pepper and oregano. Shake oil and vinegar together and drizzle on salad; toss gently. Sprinkle with Romano cheese.

66Homemade noodles are very easy to make. Some people think making noodles is a big thing, but all you need are flour, a little water, a couple of eggs and some salt. Knead the dough until it's stiff and roll it out like pie dough. Then cut it into thin strips. Some little old Italian ladies can make noodles so thin and precise that they look like they were cut by machine. My noodles aren't perfect—but at least they're homemade, and you know what you're eating.99

# Friday Night Fare

BAKED WHITE FISH

CABBAGE ROLLS WITH TOMATO SAUCE

ITALIAN SALAD D'AGOSTINO

BREAD AND BUTTER

SPUMONI ICE CREAM (PAGE 57)

*

SERVES 4 TO 6

## Baked White Fish

1 whole large white fish, cleaned (allow at least ½ pound per person)
  Salt
1 cup bread crumbs
  Salt, pepper and oregano to taste
2 cloves garlic, minced
¼ cup grated Parmesan cheese
1 egg, well beaten
  Butter
  Thin lemon slices

Rub the fish with salt inside and out, then rinse well with cold water. Mix the bread crumbs, salt, pepper, oregano, garlic and cheese thoroughly. Fill the fish, saving some stuffing for the outside. Roll the stuffed fish in egg and then in remaining bread crumb mixture. Place the fish in a greased baking pan. Dot with butter and lay lemon slices over it. Cover tightly with aluminum foil. Bake at 375° for 45 minutes.

## Cabbage Rolls with Tomato Sauce

¾ pound ground beef
2 eggs
  Grated Parmesan cheese
  Salt, pepper and oregano to taste
2 cloves garlic, minced
1½ cups cooked rice
1 medium head or 2 small heads cabbage
6 quarts boiling water
  Tomato Sauce (page 85)
  Garlic powder to taste

Mix together ground beef, eggs, ½ cup cheese, salt, pepper, oregano, minced garlic and the rice. Taste for seasoning and set aside. Remove the cabbage core. Drop the whole cabbage into boiling water and cook for 20 minutes or longer, until the leaves come apart. Drain in a colander. Take 1 large cabbage leaf at a time and put 2 tablespoons of meat mixture on it. Roll in long rolls, tucking in the ends so the stuffing doesn't fall out. Place the cabbage rolls in a greased baking pan and pour Tomato Sauce over the top. Sprinkle with more cheese, salt, pepper, oregano and the garlic powder. Bake at 375° for 1 hour.

## Tomato Sauce

2 onions, chopped
1 clove garlic, minced
¼ cup oil
1 (29-ounce) can tomato puree

Sauté onions and garlic slowly in oil. Add tomato puree and simmer for 45 minutes.

## Italian Salad D'Agostino

1 head lettuce, coarsely chopped
  Salt, pepper, oregano and minced garlic to taste
2 tomatoes, cut into wedges
¼ cup oil
1 tablespoon wine vinegar

Arrange lettuce in individual bowls. Add salt, pepper, oregano and garlic. Garnish with tomato wedges. Mix oil and vinegar together and drizzle over the salad.

Note: Make a little extra dressing to serve with the salad for those who like more dressing.

66 When you're cooking a whole fish, make sure you wash the inside of it thoroughly. Any membrane will add bad flavor to your fish. Wash the cavity with salt and then rinse with cold water.

Don't you *dare* have a bland fish. Season your fish with salt, pepper, oregano and garlic. 99

# Not Just Meat and Potatoes

ROAST LOIN OF PORK WITH
POTATOES

PEAS WITH ONIONS

GREEN BEAN AND
MUSHROOM SALAD

RICE PUDDING

*

SERVES 4

## Roast Loin of Pork with Potatoes

   3- to 4-pound pork loin roast
¼  cup oil
   Salt to taste
½  teaspoon pepper
¼  teaspoon oregano
 2  cloves garlic, minced
 3  sprigs parsley, chopped
 2  cups water
 6  potatoes, halved

Rub pork with oil and season with salt, pepper, oregano and garlic; place in a roasting pan. Roast in a 350° oven for 2½ hours or until done. One hour before meat is done, add water and potatoes to the pan; baste often. Add more seasonings, according to your taste.

## Peas with Onions

¼  cup oil
 2  small onions, sliced
 1  (16-ounce) can peas
    (undrained)
    Salt and pepper to taste

Heat oil in saucepan. Sauté onions until light golden brown. Add peas, salt and pepper. Simmer slowly for 15 minutes.

## Green Bean and Mushroom Salad

 1  pound green beans, cooked,
    or 1 (16-ounce) can green
    beans, drained
 1  small onion, thinly sliced
 1  clove garlic, minced
 1  (4-ounce) can button
    mushrooms
    Salt and pepper to taste
¼  cup oil
    Juice of 1 lemon
¼  cup grated Romano cheese

Put beans in a bowl. Add onion, garlic and mushrooms. Season with salt and pepper. Mix oil and lemon juice and sprinkle over beans; toss lightly. Sprinkle with cheese.

## Rice Pudding

⅔  cup uncooked rice
 2  cups water
 3  cups milk
 5  egg yolks
 1  cup sugar
 1  teaspoon salt
 1  teaspoon cinnamon

Add rice to water and milk and simmer until rice is soft. (Do not bring water and milk to boil before adding rice.) Beat egg yolks and sugar until fluffy. Gradually stir in the rice, mix well and return to saucepan. Add salt and cook for about 2 more minutes, stirring constantly. Pour into pudding dishes; sprinkle with cinnamon.

## Mama D's Hot Dog Stew

¼ cup oil
2 small onions, diced
2 cloves garlic, minced
⅛ teaspoon pepper
⅛ teaspoon oregano
    Salt to taste
1 teaspoon basil
1 pound hot dogs, cut into
    1-inch pieces
3 small potatoes, peeled and
    quartered
4 carrots, sliced
1 (29-ounce) can peas
    (undrained)
2 stalks celery, sliced
3 or 4 ripe tomatoes, crushed

Heat oil in a saucepan and add onions, garlic, pepper, oregano, salt and basil. Sauté until onions are golden brown. In a roasting pan, place hot dogs, potatoes, carrots, peas, celery and tomatoes. Add sautéed onions and toss together lightly. Bake in a 350° oven at least 1¼ hours, until all the vegetables are tender.

## Pickled Pepper Salad

2 cups sliced green and red
    peppers (may be diced
    instead, if you like)
1 cup chopped celery
½ cup Italian green or black
    olives
1 (2-ounce) can anchovies,
    drained, or 2 tablespoons
    capers
    Salt, pepper and oregano to
    taste
1 clove garlic, crushed
3 tablespoons oil
1 tablespoon wine vinegar

Put peppers, celery, olives, anchovies, salt, pepper, oregano and garlic into a serving bowl. Add oil and vinegar and toss lightly.

## Orange and Apple Slices in Wine

Slice peeled oranges and apples very thinly. Put in small fruit bowls and sprinkle with a little sugar to taste. Pour Marsala wine or your favorite wine over the fruit slices. Chill in refrigerator for at least 1 hour before serving.

# Savory and Low-Cost

**MAMA D'S HOT DOG STEW**

**PICKLED PEPPER SALAD**

**BREAD AND BUTTER**

**ORANGE AND APPLE SLICES IN WINE**

\*

**SERVES 4 TO 6**

# Turkey for the Holidays

**ROAST TURKEY**
**ROAST POTATOES**
**BROCCOLI WITH PARMESAN**
**ANCHOVY-ROMAINE SALAD**
**BREAD AND BUTTER**
**PEARS IN WINE**
**HONEY COOKIES**

*

**SERVES 6**

## Roast Turkey

12- to 15-pound turkey
   Salt
  3 onions, chopped
  2 cloves garlic, minced
  ½ cup oil
  2 cups diced celery
  1 pound ground beef
  1 teaspoon fennel seed
 15 slices dry bread, soaked in water and squeezed
  3 eggs
  ¾ cup grated Romano cheese
  4 sprigs parsley, chopped
   Salt, pepper, oregano and minced garlic to taste
  ½ cup (¼ pound) butter

Wash turkey inside and out. Rub with salt and rinse well, especially the cavity. Dry with paper towels.

Brown onions and 2 cloves garlic, minced, in hot oil. Remove to a large bowl. Add celery to hot oil and cook for 5 minutes; place in the bowl. Mix beef with fennel seed and cook lightly for 10 minutes. Place in bowl along with bread, eggs, cheese, parsley, salt, pepper and oregano; mix gently.

Melt butter over low heat and season with more salt, pepper, oregano and minced garlic. Brush turkey cavity with the butter, fill with dressing and truss. Brush outside of turkey with remaining butter. Place in a roasting pan and cover with aluminum foil. Roast in a 325° oven 25 minutes per pound. One hour before turkey is done, remove foil and continue roasting until golden brown.

## Roast Potatoes

 6 large potatoes, peeled
 ½ cup oil
 1 teaspoon rosemary
   Salt to taste
 ½ teaspoon pepper
 ¼ teaspoon oregano
 4 sprigs parsley, chopped
 2 cloves garlic, minced

Cut potatoes into quarters. Put in baking dish with oil and seasonings. Gently toss together. Bake, stirring occasionally, in a 325° oven for 1 hour or until tender when pierced with a fork.

## Broccoli with Parmesan

1 large head broccoli
  Salt, pepper and oregano to
  taste
¼ teaspoon garlic powder or 2
  cloves garlic, minced
3 tablespoons oil
3 tablespoons grated Parmesan
  cheese
  Lemon wedges

Wash broccoli, peel stems and trim tough ends. Cut into pieces. Cook in salted boiling water until tender; drain. Sprinkle with salt, pepper, oregano, garlic, oil and cheese. Serve with lemon wedges.

## Anchovy-Romaine Salad

1 large head romaine lettuce
1 clove garlic, minced
1 onion, finely chopped
4 radishes, thinly sliced
1 (2-ounce) can anchovies,
  drained and chopped
1 tablespoon grated Romano
  cheese
  Salt to taste
½ teaspoon pepper
2 tablespoons oil
1 egg
  Juice of 1 lemon

Mix all ingredients except egg and lemon juice in a bowl. Break egg over salad, add lemon juice and toss gently.

## Pears in Wine

1 (29-ounce) can pear halves
  (undrained)
4 whole cloves
1 stick cinnamon
1 cup wine (red or white)

Put pears in a bowl. Add cloves, cinnamon and wine. Chill; serve cold, in sherbet glasses.

## Honey Cookies

1 cup oil
1 cup water or dry wine
1 teaspoon salt
2 cups flour
  Oil for frying
  Honey
  Granulated sugar

Heat oil, water and salt in saucepan until lukewarm. Remove from heat and add flour, a little at a time, mixing in thoroughly. Roll dough out into a rope shape, 1½ inches thick. Cut into ¾-inch pieces. Press each piece on fine side of cheese grater with thumb to make a design. Fry in oil until golden brown. Drain on paper towels. Roll in honey and sprinkle with granulated sugar while still hot. Makes about 3 dozen cookies.

66 Make your own bread crumbs; they'll be much better than the ones you buy in the supermarket. Dry your stale bread in the oven. Grate it and keep it in a covered jar in the refrigerator. It lasts forever. If you wish, you can season it to taste.

And don't throw out stale cake or cookie crumbs. Grind them up and mix them with cream frosting and use for coffee cake filling. It makes the best coffee cake filling there is. 99

# Saturday Night Supper

**SWEET AND SOUR MEATBALLS**
**STUFFED TOMATOES**
**ROMAINE LETTUCE SALAD**
**BREAD AND BUTTER**
**COFFEE ICE CREAM**

*

**SERVES 4**

## Sweet and Sour Meatballs

1 pound ground beef
½ pound ground pork
3 eggs, beaten
½ cup grated Romano cheese
2 cloves garlic, minced
3 or 4 sprigs parsley, chopped, or 1 teaspoon dried parsley
    Salt to taste
½ teaspoon fennel seeds
¼ teaspoon oregano
½ teaspoon pepper
4 or 5 slices bread, soaked in water and squeezed as dry as possible
3 onions, chopped
1 (6-ounce) can tomato paste
1½ cups water
½ cup wine vinegar
2 tablespoons brown sugar
    Salt to taste
½ teaspoon pepper

Mix first 11 ingredients together and shape into balls. Place on a greased baking pan with low sides and bake in a 375° oven for 30 to 40 minutes, until meatballs are browned all over.

Put drippings from baked meatballs in a large saucepan. Sauté onions. Add tomato paste, water, vinegar, sugar, salt and ½ teaspoon pepper. Stir well. Add meatballs and simmer slowly for 1 hour.

## Stuffed Tomatoes

4 large ripe tomatoes
1 cup water or soup stock
½ cup uncooked rice
1 (2-ounce) can anchovies, drained and chopped
    Pinch of salt
¼ teaspoon pepper
¼ cup grated Romano cheese
2 tablespoons butter, melted
½ cup grated mozzarella cheese
2 tablespoons oil
1 clove garlic, minced

Hollow out tomatoes. Bring water to a boil; cook rice. Drain and place in a bowl. Add anchovies, salt, pepper, Romano cheese and butter. (Add tomato pulp, too, if you wish.) Toss gently. Fill hollowed tomatoes with rice mixture. Sprinkle mozzarella cheese over each filled tomato. In a small baking dish, heat oil with garlic. Add stuffed tomatoes and bake in a 375° oven for 15 minutes.

## Romaine Lettuce Salad

1  head romaine lettuce
   Salt to taste
¼  teaspoon pepper
⅛  teaspoon oregano
1  clove garlic, minced
¼  cup oil
1  tablespoon wine vinegar

Separate lettuce leaves; rinse and pat dry with paper towels. Break leaves into serving pieces in a salad bowl. Season with salt, pepper, oregano and garlic. Mix oil and vinegar and pour over lettuce. Toss gently.

## Coffee Ice Cream

1  cup espresso coffee
2  cups whipping cream
4  eggs, beaten
1½  cups sugar
   Whipped cream

Combine coffee and whipping cream. Heat to boiling point. Cool slightly. Slowly add eggs and sugar. Mix thoroughly. Cook, uncovered, over low heat, stirring constantly, until mixture is thick. Cool, then freeze. Serve in sherbet glasses, topped with whipped cream.

"Don't season your food at the table. Then it's too late. It has to be done in your kitchen. Food has so much more flavor if the seasonings are cooked right into it. *Anybody* can add more salt after the food is on the table!"

# Tasty and Thrifty

SAUTEED CHICKEN GIZZARDS
EGGPLANT CASSEROLE
CUCUMBER SALAD
BREAD AND BUTTER
LADYFINGERS

*

SERVES 6

## Sautéed Chicken Gizzards

¼ cup oil
2 small onions, thinly sliced
Pinch of salt
½ teaspoon pepper
2 cloves garlic, minced
2 tablespoons finely chopped parsley
½ teaspoon nutmeg
2 pounds chicken gizzards
1 (29-ounce) can Italian tomatoes, crushed

Heat oil in a saucepan. Add onions, salt, pepper, garlic, parsley and nutmeg; sauté until onions and garlic are golden brown. Rinse gizzards; pat dry with paper towels. Add to saucepan and sauté for 5 minutes. Add tomatoes and simmer slowly until gizzards are tender, about 45 minutes to 1 hour.

## Eggplant Casserole

1 large eggplant
2 small zucchini
1 large onion, sliced
2 small tomatoes, crushed
Salt to taste
¼ teaspoon pepper
¼ teaspoon oregano
2 cloves garlic, minced
½ cup grated Romano cheese
½ cup grated mozzarella cheese
¼ cup oil

Pare and slice eggplant. Cut zucchini into quarters. Grease a baking dish and put in a layer of eggplant, a layer of onion slices and a layer of zucchini. Cover with crushed tomatoes. Season with a little salt, pepper, oregano and garlic. Sprinkle with some of the Romano and mozzarella cheeses. Repeat layers until all ingredients are used (reserve some of the cheese for the top). Pour oil over all and sprinkle with remaining cheese. Cover; bake in a 375° oven for about 50 minutes; then bake uncovered for 5 to 10 minutes, until vegetables are tender.

## Cucumber Salad

2 large cucumbers, unpeeled
2 cloves garlic, minced
  Salt to taste
¼ teaspoon pepper
⅛ teaspoon oregano
¼ cup oil
1 tablespoon wine vinegar

Scrub cucumbers and slice thinly. Add garlic. Season with salt, pepper and oregano. Mix oil and vinegar and pour over all. Chill before serving.

## Ladyfingers

4 eggs
1 teaspoon almond extract
½ cup sugar
⅔ cup cake flour
½ teaspoon salt
2 teaspoons baking powder

Separate eggs. Beat yolks until fluffy; beat in almond extract. In a separate bowl, beat egg whites until stiff. Add sugar to egg whites and beat again. Fold in egg yolks. Sift together cake flour, salt and baking powder and fold into other ingredients. Drop by tablespoons onto ungreased cookie sheet, forming finger shapes. Bake in a preheated 375° oven about 10 minutes, until light brown. Remove immediately and cool on rack. Makes about 4 dozen.

66 You can't save on your rent or electricity, or when you need to buy a pair of shoes. But if you learn to fill your cooking pots, you can save money on food. I had one friend who'd throw away so much food that I'd retrieve it right away and cook it for her, to show her what she could do with it. 99

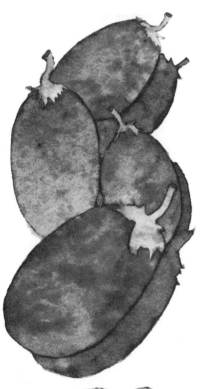

# Index

Fettuccine, 28, 68
Filled cookies, Mama D's, 35
Finger croquettes, 12
Fish. *See names of fish.*
Flounder, baked fillet of, 28
Fondue, cheese, Italian, 56
Fontina (cheese)
  and pepper salad, 83
  fruit and, 48
  Italian cheese fondue, 56
Frankfurters (hot dog stew), 87
French bread cubes, 56
French fried onion rings, 31
Fritters
  almond ricotta cheese, 19
  apple, 69
  celery, 7
  zucchini, 8
Frosted grapes, 21
Frozen peaches, 41
Fruit. *See also names of fruits.*
  and Fontina, 48
  Macedonia, 40
  plate, Sicilian, 23

Garlic bread, 71
  Parmesan, 23
  sautéed, 18
Gnocchi, 66
Grapes
  Bibb lettuce salad with, 29
  frosted, 21
Green bean(s). *See* Bean(s).
Green noodles (spinach noodles), 82
Green peppers. *See* Pepper(s).
Greens, mustard, boiled, 33

Honey
  clusters, 37
  cookies, 89
Hot dog stew, Mama D's, 87

Ice
  lemon, 53
  strawberry, 17
Ice cream
  biscuit tortoni, 59
  coffee, 91
  spumoni, 57
Italian
  cheese fondue, 56
  rum cake, 81
  salads. *See* Salad.

Italian style
  baked potatoes, 78
  liver, 14
  meat loaf, 62
  new potatoes, 8

Kidneys, veal, sautéed, 48

Ladyfingers, 93
Lamb, roast, Sicilian style, 24
Lasagne, baked, 22
Lemon
  cake, 77
  ice, 53
Lentil
  salad, 24
  soup, 42
Lettuce salads. *See* Salad.
Linguine, 45
Liver, Italian-style, 14
Lobster fra diavolo, 54

Macaroons, 55
Marinated steak, 36
Mashed potatoes Romano, 62
Meat. *See* Beef; Lamb; Pork; Veal.
Meat loaf Italian style, 62
Meatballs, sweet and sour, 90
Milanese risotto, 52
Minestrone, 64
Mostaccioli, duck with, 74
Mushrooms with garlic and onion, 72.
    *See also* Salad.
Mustard greens, boiled, 33

Noodles, spinach, with ragu sauce, 82

Olive salads, 9, 65
Onion(s)
  and beet salad, 11
  and tomato salad with Roquefort, 15
  rings, French fried, 31
  tomato and pepper salad, 47
Orange
  and apple slices in wine, 87
  salad, 7
Oven-baked beef stew, 65

Parmesan garlic bread, 23
Pasta. *See names of pasta.*

Peaches
  and wine, 81
  frozen, 41
  with Marsala, 51
Pear(s)
  in wine, 89
  lettuce and nut salad, 13
  stuffed with Gorgonzola, 32
  with red wine, 11
Peas
  and tomatoes, pasta shells with, 14
  with onions, 86
  with prosciutto, 62
  with rice, 49
Pepper(s)
  and Fontina cheese salad, 83
  pickled, salad, 87
  stuffed, 16
  tomato and onion salad, 47
Pickled pepper salad, 87
Pie
  apple, old-fashioned, 65
  ricotta, 29
Piedmont-style rice, 10
Pizza, 50
Polenta with sausage, 41
Pompano, baked, 10
Pork. *See also* Sausage(s).
  chop suey, Mama D's, 26
  chops Neapolitan style, 78
  loin of, roast, with potatoes, 86
  meat loaf Italian style, 62
  meatballs, sweet and sour, 90
  shanks with tomato sauce, 68
  spareribs, barbecued, 20, 60
Pot roast with vegetables, 40
Potato(es)
  and bean salad, 58
  baked
    Italian style, 78
    with mozzarella cheese, 16
  boiled, with parsley, 24
  curly endive salad, 71
  finger croquettes, 12
  fried, Romano, 21
  gnocchi, 66
  mashed, Romano, 62
  new, Italian-style, 8
  roast, 88
  spicy, 47
  stuffed eggplant and, 76
Pudding
  almond bread, 61
  caramel, 27
  rice, 86
  ricotta (cheese), 9, 75

**95**

EF